Coast of Teeth

Travels to English Seaside Towns in an Age of Anxiety

First published in 2023 by
Signal Books Limited
36 Minster Road
Oxford
OX4 1LY
www.signalbooks.co.uk

A catalogue record for this book is available from the British Library.

ISBN 978-1-8384630-7-6 Paper

Production: Louis Netter
Cover Design: Louis Netter
Illustrations: Louis Netter
Printed in the UK by 4edge Ltd

Preface

Since it's never a good idea to baffle your readers as soon as they open your book, we feel we should explain our unusual title. While researching Côte d'Ivoire a few years ago, Tom found the phrase 'Coast of Teeth' in an obscure 18th century British travelogue. He realised it must have been a sloppy mistranslation of 'Ivory Coast'. White people had yet to formally steal that part of West Africa, but were already shooting its elephants. When Tom mentioned the phrase to Louis during the planning stages of this book, he felt it had a visual and auditory charm. Though the original meaning of 'Coast of Teeth' had nothing to do with English seaside towns, we decided to make it our title for a book about English seaside towns anyway.

Nominative determinism ensued. Teeth became a recurring motif of our fieldwork. We found debris and buildings and rock formations that looked like fangs, molars and incisors. More literally, our beach-combing friends inform us that dentures often wash up on shores. Stretching the definition a bit, some beachside burgs have a figurative bite to them, given the aggressive disaffection felt by their denizens. The more conservative coast-dwellers we've met see themselves as protecting their island enclave from refugees and other intruders, just as an animal's sharp teeth defends it from predators.

Our itinerary was not entirely rational either. Time and budget constraints meant limiting our beat to English seaside towns rather than British ones. (In our defence, the English coastline is the 30th longest in the world, so plenty to see there.) For similar reasons we failed to visit such iconic places as Brighton and Margate, which may be unforgivable in the eyes of littoral lovers. However, there's plenty of variety to the towns we did get to, as hopefully you will agree when you read about them right about now.

T.S. & L.N.

Contents

Introduction: Coastal Curiosities

The first Covid lockdown literally narrowed people's horizons. Travel addicts – the authors of this book included – were constrained to hour-long outings within a few miles' radius. (Of course, not everyone followed the rules.) We, who between us had covered masses of ground across all five continents, watched in terror as our worlds shrunk to a couple of neighbourhoods in a couple of towns in southern England. The novelty and variety that are travel's allures were usurped by the boredom of repetition and the contempt that familiarity breeds. And once outside we couldn't interact with others – we believe that human encounters make up 99% of travel's appeal. In a society that was already atomised, people now had more reason to avoid each other. It's easier to elude eye contact or pretend not to have noticed someone if you're both wearing masks. The risk of appearing rude when you cross the road to avoid a mean-looking character is reduced when you have the alibi of not wanting to spread a lethal disease.

At the claustrophobic nadir of that first lockdown, we talked longingly of going somewhere, anywhere, and documenting it. Once restrictions were eased, international travel remained too much of a hassle for most Britons.

If you can't have a beach break in the tropical heat, one in less-than-tropical Weston or Whitby is a reasonable plan B. And so in summer 2021 there was a boom in 'staycations' along the English coast.

However, to quote the late great comic Bill Hicks, 'What's the fucking deal with the beach? It's where dirt meets water.' Why throughout history have seaside towns been so seductive? They weren't always. As Kathryn Ferry in her book *Seaside 100* explains, until well into the 18th century Britons viewed the ocean with a mix of fear and repugnance, not least because it was where invaders tended to come from. This all changed when doctors recommended bathing in salty water to heal ailments from gout to melancholy, rabies to broken legs. The upper crust duly descended on the likes of Margate and Scarborough.

It was in the middle Victorian years that such places started to resemble today's vision of the seaside-as-leisure-amenity. Railway expansion and the introduction of bank holidays turned the coastal vacation into a golden goose – or seagull. The 1860s to the 1890s – a relatively short period – saw the birth of piers, grand hotels, amusement arcades, beach huts, promenade shelters, fish and chips, souvenir rock candy, deck chairs, band stands, aquariums, Punch and Judy shows and so much else that fits our very model of a modern seaside town. The next wave of innovations came in the 1920s and 30s – ice cream cones, mass-produced buckets and spades, double decker promenades, Butlin's holiday camps, surfing, sun-tan lotion and palm trees. Whereas most of these features have lasted into the present, reenergised by nostalgia or irony, others rightly haven't. Displaying premature babies in incubators on promenades – as seen on the Prohibition-era TV drama *Boardwalk Empire* – went out of fashion during the war. Not since the 1950s have there been freak shows starring very short, very thin or very overweight people. Nor would the Elephant Man, the Balloon-Headed Baby and the 'half-man, half-woman' be acceptable today. That said, other conventions that died off on dry land live on along that curious border between dirt and water. When we joined that post-lockdown exodus to the beach, we were confronted with museums stocking wares long past their political sell-by-dates – and not just toy gollies.*

Aside from Covid and casual racism, we came face-to-face with other social problems. The English beach holiday has been wilting since the 1970s. Many seaside economies are now in tatters. More recently, austerity policies have pulled down life expectancy and cranked up the rate of chronic disease amongst coastal populations. Frustrations about poverty, lack of opportunities and being left behind may have fuelled Brexit. Political analyst Chris Hanretty has found that around 100 of the 120 or so constituencies with a coastline voted to leave the EU. Research by the University of Aberdeen revealed that 92% of fishing industry workers voted the same way.

Our land's edges are also on the business end of climate breakdown. Rising sea levels mean more flooding. If something isn't done soon, Southsea will be underwater in 40 years' time, scientists warn. In Scarborough and elsewhere, cliff erosion is already pushing buildings into Davy Jones' Locker. None of this is helped by corporations blithely dumping sewage. Parts of the Solent aren't safe to swim in and – if you're a smaller creature – not fit to live in. We wanted to see for ourselves the damage done by plastic pollution that's killing off wildlife and turning beauty spots into eyesores – while we still could.

In addition to reporting on these gritty realities, we've tried to understand how the English littoral is perceived and imagined. Seaside towns are not only geographically but socially and culturally far from England's land-locked heart and the myths attached to it – village cricket, rolling meadows, 'Old London Town' and so forth. Modern travel and psychogeographical writing has tended to spotlight what we've dubbed 'inland England'. This includes

Robert Macfarlane's fascination for ancient rural byways or Alan Moore's preoccupation with his hometown of Northampton because it is, he argues, 'right at the centre of the country, and so all of England's inner conflicts have more or less passed through it.' Those other chroniclers of inland England, Iain Sinclair and Nick Papadimitriou, have a penchant for 'edgelands' that muddy the boundaries between country and city. With the exception of Will Self, such psychogeographers are not as interested in the damp far reaches of our island.

But we think that seaside towns, too, are liminal spaces given their hazy situation between land and sea, metropole and periphery, home and abroad. This 'in-betweenness' makes for contradictions between wealth and poverty, frivolity and misery, familiarity and alienness, past and present, fact and fantasy. Bournemouth's astronomical house prices and ageing population contrast starkly with its excess of rehab clinics and substance-related deaths. Torquay, Scarborough and Southsea's architecture has been fragmented into an uncanny jumble of historical eras and cultural themes. And almost all shoreline settlements are trapped in the culinary timewarp of the transatlantic 1950s: milkshakes, burgers, hot dogs, pulled pork, endless cups of coffee, endless cups of tea, full English breakfasts, bacon sandwiches, teacakes,

scones. Such quirks are some distance – spatially and visually – from the uniformity of the English interior and its interchangeable 'everytowns', as the philosopher Julian Baggini terms them, of retail citadels, fast food factories and red-brick estates. In an increasingly globalised and standardised world could seaside towns be amongst the last outposts of oddity, individuality and the eccentrically pass?

We found out the stressful way that seaside towns, sited as they are away from metropolitan centres of education and the media, can be incubators for fringe delusions. We've seen far too much anti-vax graffiti in Dorset and are in no hurry to return to Torquay's Real Crime Museum and its Princess Diana-related conspiracy theorising. Other towns with current and historical links to the armed forces are being infected with new variants of chauvinism, nationalism and militarism, arguably nurtured by Brexit and Britain's new imperial gumption (expressed through its largest defence spending increase since the Cold War and its naval sabre-rattling against China). Although it's been a resort since the early 1800s, Southsea has long been surrounded by a large navy base, barracks and coastal turrets, some dating back to medieval times. This hostile geography has fed a suspicious 'island mentality' and, at times, paranoia about foreign invasion. While lately Southsea's demographics

Isle of Wight
2020

have altered enough so that its first ever Labour MP could be elected, xenophobic and anti-immigration attitudes remain strong, channelled by demagogic Conservative politicians. If some seaside towns are literal (littoral) and metaphorical bulwarks against the rest of the world, others 'import' unusual facets of foreign culture. This is true of Jaywick and St Osyth in southeast Essex, where trailer parks and shanty-style dwellings lacking mains gas or electricity resemble a 'Global South' slum.

Aside from the difficulties of conceptualising seaside towns, there were more practical obstacles to overcome. When we started our travels in April 2021, there was still enough Covid about to complicate everything from catching a train to queuing for breakfast. We'd turn up at attractions to find them shut down by the pandemic. But as some avenues closed others opened. Unable to access the big draws, we refocused on less obvious yet equally interesting details – graffiti, signage, road names, memorial plaques on benches, characters in pubs and on street corners, the resurgence of coastal activities from beach-combing to metal detecting, and a lot else. In some ways this book is a paean to the marginal and the marginalised, the obscure and the outlandish, the lesser-known and the under-reported. The English seaside specialises in these phenomena.

Such encounters were enabled by our loose methodology. In each of the twenty-one towns we covered, we took what psychogeographers call a dérive– a long, spontaneous walk for distances of up to eight miles. This invited chance into the reportage process. We stumbled on people and places we wouldn't have otherwise.

In our research on the seaside that complemented our legwork, we tried to avoid forming preconceptions. This was important when covering needier communities. We have striven to represent them fairly, accurately and empathetically – unlike tabloid stories and TV shows on the 'Broken Britain' of feckless, drunken, violent and sweary 'left-behinds'. This 'poverty porn' doesn't bother to analyse the situation; it exists for the titillation of the middle-class voyeur.

Though this book is not a sociological investigation, we've done our best as storytellers to explain the social and political contexts of the struggles and suffering we've witnessed. From Scarborough to Clacton to Boscombe, underfunding, underskilling, unemployment and flaws in the benefits system have made life miserable for multitudes. Though a secondary aim was to raise awareness about the challenges facing the English seaside today, our main motive to do this book was curiosity. We're fascinated by the social and cultural quirks of seaside towns. More than that, this is personal. We've both worked for ten years in a seaside town, have lived in them at various times and Tom spent his formative years getting frustrated in two. Whatever the nature of your own curiosity about the English seaside, we hope this book will sate it.

Tom Sykes and Louis Netter
March 2023

* We've decided to use the term 'golly' instead of more offensive alternatives referring to the notorious racist caricatures.

THE WEST
Myths Minor and Major
Torquay and Paignton

Cruising through the West Country, Louis and I are shocked by the graffiti on motorway flyovers – MOCKDOWN; LEFT LIE VIRUS; BBC VIRUS; OUR FEAR IS THEIR POWER. This turns out to be useful preparation for the strange ideas Torquay has in store for us.

Our first impression is good though. Palm trees and parasol-shadowed cafés spin past us on the M5 into town, while the Art Decoish Pierre Bistrot restaurant and attached walkway curve above our heads, silver silhouettes against a pre-noon sun that's brightening to blinding-point. In the marina that takes a U-shaped bite out of the town centre, we gaze up at a rocky height of stucco condominiums that could be Marseille or Cádiz. But the buildings below them don't feel very Southern European. There's the Torquay Pavilion's Anglo-Indian domes, a typically seasidey big wheel, a modernistic church. A peeling, vacant Debenhams has fallen victim to the slow death of England's high streets. It's a motley skyline with no common theme or architectural period.

Everywhere signs shout 'The English Riviera'. The one time I've heard that phrase before, I'm sure it was meant ironically. The actor John Cleese used it to describe Torquay's charms, prompting high-pitched canned laughter, in the seventies sitcom *Fawlty Towers*, about a disaster-prone hotel in the same town. In the minds of many, Torquay is associated with the perpetually panicked character of Basil Fawlty. He seems less funny as time goes by, given his class snobbery, mild misogyny, less mild xenophobia and range of unacknowledged mental disorders from pathological lying to grand delusion.

While our hotel is better run than *Fawlty Towers*, the average age of its

guests is similar. The ubiquity of limps, breathing conditions and walking sticks mean slow-footed queues for reception, the bar and the restaurant. The delays can't all be blamed on old age – the hotel is fully booked due to the recent lifting of Covid travel restrictions. The crowd makes distancing tough. I overhear talk of grandchildren, a shop that can send clotted cream by post and Torquay's annual hosting of a spiritualism convention. The dominant accent is Brummieish. We learn later from a Wolverhampton-born taxi driver that Torquay attracts Midlanders for no other reason than its closeness.

The hotel's lounge is a shabby stab at manorial grandeur. Over-varnished pillars stand tiredly over cracked mosaic flooring. There's a pool table in lieu of a billiards one. The frayed settees must date back to the *Fawlty Towers* era. A corny portrait of the Queen and Prince Philip hangs askew above the fake fireplace.

We schlep down a steep cliffside path in an area called Daddyhole. Now there's a *double entendre* for a seaside postcard. Ahead of us, a trendily dressed boomer couple tell us to be careful going down. I lean over and note how sheer the descent becomes. It looks about as perilous as going first in a game of Russian Roulette... involving a fully loaded Tommy gun.

From where we're standing now is a vista not to be missed: a gargantuan crag slowly collapsing, spilling itself into the ocean rock-by-rock. It reminds me of an old man's profile – jagged, wrinkled, dribbling – staring out to sea at some wave-borne menace. In a small island-nation like Britain, the

main menace today is rising sea levels and our coast is literally the last line of defence. Further out to sea, three cruise liners look to be advancing towards us, but in truth they're moored up while their passengers explore Torquay. At any rate, given how much these ships' pollution contributes to erosion, they may as well be a naval flotilla shelling our stony old admiral of a rock face.

The next morning we're on Victoria Parade before some very different boats at the marina. We sit outside Jack's, an American-themed diner that's conceded to local tastes by serving West Country cream teas alongside greasy, meaty, carby classics from much further to the west. Of course, the connections between the US and the south of England go back way before the fifties, with the first settlers of the New World coming from ports like Plymouth and Southampton.

Since then the cultural traffic has been going the other way. Many of the quintessential traits of the English seaside in fact come from the United States. Not just burgers and hot dogs (themselves originally from deeper into Europe), but crazy golf, big band concerts, ice cream parlours, felt cowboy hats with phrases on them like KISS ME QUICK and electro-mechanical arcade machines with appetising titles such as 'The Electric Chair'. Though pinball probably began in the Middle Ages, the flippers and flashing lights of the pastime as we know it today were imported from America in the 1930s. While nothing so dodgy ever happened in the UK, the US pinball industry came to be a front business for organised crime, prompting New York City mayor La Guardia to ban it and destroy 2,000 machines in 1942.

To a nationalist's further chagrin, certain ingredients of the full English breakfast also hail from across the pond. Baked beans were created by H.J. Heinz Company of Pittsburgh in the 1880s but have since been more popular in the UK. Heinz started peddling ketchup here around the same time. Hash browns are thought to have emerged in New York at the tail-end of the 19th century.

It gets worse for anyone who still thinks there's anything culturally pure-bred about our seaside. Fish and chips is a case of cross-pollination – the fish was first fried by Jewish immigrants in Elizabethan times, the chips by the French in the late 1700s. Flip-flops were invented in Japan to help kickstart rubber production after World War II. But doesn't the name sound so English? The deckchair was born in the Raj, pioneered by puttee-clad colonial soldiers to make jungle camping comfy.

Other businesses along Victoria Parade and Beacon Hill allude to the Indian subcontinent and other parts of the world once oppressed by the British that have now been domesticated into symbols of our love of eating, drinking and just feeling good. Two Indian restaurants. An Irish pub. An holistic yoga centre.

With anti-lockdown slogans still ringing in my ears, I'm curious about the 'Princess Diana conspiracy theories' on the pavement sign for Torquay's 'world famous' True Crime Museum. Its address is aptly sinister: in a backstreet behind Victoria Parade, down some ill-lit steps under a sordid neon sign flashing OPEN.

The receptionist is also appropri-ate for the place. An ex-con caricature, his long hair is gelled back into a pony-tail. He sniffs and shivers druggily while explaining that the museum is owned by the son of Charles Bronson – not the Hollywood actor but the Luton-born hoodlum who's been banged up since 1974 for causing mayhem in every prison he's been in. The museum is no bigger than a bedsit, yet a sign asks patrons to allow an hour for it. This inaccuracy is minor compared to the permanent exhibition of video screens, newspapers, books and photographs claiming that Princess Diana was vari-ously murdered by the British security state, the Royal Family or Dodi Fayed's business rivals. While there have been high-level conspiracies – Jimmy Savile, Jeffrey Epstein and the case for certain wars the UK has fought spring to mind – the 'evidence' here doesn't persuade me there was one to do away with Di. Equally dubious is the campaigning tone of the Bron-son pieces. They urge that, like Man-dela or the Birmingham Six, he's the victim of a miscarriage of justice. (He has watertight convictions for armed robbery, wounding with intent, criminal damage and false imprisonment). Even so, the intended sincerity of the cam-paign is undermined by the preposter-

ous waxwork model of Bronson, whose white suit, wavy moustache and bowler hat make him look more like a 1920s Parisian mime artist than the tough-nut that glares from tabloid spreads, true crime book covers and the 2008 biopic starring Tom Hardy.

I leave, bewildered by how such a temple of disinformation can operate without controversy or regulation. We find a more directly dangerous form of propaganda in the unlikely environs of Paignton, another shoreline settlement three miles along Torbay. The promenade leading there takes us past kids buried in the sand to their waists and to a public toilet with a poster in ominous red font:

15 YEAR OLD BOY DIES OF HEART ATTACK TWO DAYS AFTER TAKING PFIZER VACCINE HAD NO HISTORY OF ALLERGIC REACTIONS

Next to it is a smaller sticker with a cartoon of a nervous, sweating, masked man trapped in a translucent box with an ambulance light on top of it. On the sides of the box are signs warning GO AWAY and STAY BACK. Above and below the whole picture it says SAVE LIVES and STOP LIVING.

The next day we discover that Torquay Museum, too, indulges in deception, but not on the scale of those hare-brained posters. One of the museum's Venetian-Gothic mezzanines (erected 1874) bigs up Torquay's most

famous daughter, Agatha Christie. She was born and grew up in the town, and locations such as the Imperial Hotel and Princess Gardens appear in her novels. Beyond that, Torquay's impact on her work is nebulous – Hercule Poirot's 'nationality may have been inspired' by Belgian immigrants she met in the town, so the website puts it. She set many more of her stories far

from Torquay – in London, Iraq, the Caribbean, on the Nile, on the Orient Express. Yet neither these tenuous links nor her reactionary worldview (look up the original title of her 1939 novel *And Then There Were None*) have prevented Torquay from cashing in on an annual literary festival in her name.

In the same questionable spirit, the museum claims several explorers as famous sons. 57 years before he

disappeared in 1925 trying to find 'Z', a mythical city of vast gold reserves and hieroglyphics-embossed temples, Percy Fawcett was born in Torquay. But that's where his connections to the town end. There's no proof it influenced his adult activities. He schooled in Teignbridge, attended the Royal Military Academy in Greenwich and spent the rest of his days in Hong Kong, Ceylon, Malta, South America and France.

You can't fault a tourist industry for exaggerating its locale's ties to the great and the good – should you wish to call Percy Fawcett that.

It's a 20-minute walk northeast from the museum to Torquay's most popular draw, that isn't really a draw. These days it's a ziggurat retirement home called Sachs Lodge, the name an easy clue to its pop culture pedigree. The moment Louis and I appear on the tarmac forecourt, two uniformed women race out to meet us with some brochures. It's as if they're expecting us. 'We're always expecting *someone*,' smiles one of them. From Tokyo to Tucson there are such militant fans of *Fawlty Towers* that they'll travel all the way to Torquay to stare at a building that stands in the place of the now-demolished Gleneagles Hotel. The Gleneagles' ill-mannered owner was reputedly John Cleese's inspiration for Basil Fawlty. If this doesn't sound like an already shaky link for Torquay to capitalise on, the show itself wasn't filmed anywhere near here. The iconic exteriors of the intro were shot in Berkshire, while the interiors were done in London studios. It's like a deviation of the Theseus' ship paradox, where philosophers speculate at what point does an object stop being that object if enough of its attributes change. How much of *Fawlty Towers* has anything to do with Torquay? Yet, in the popular imagination the two are inextricable.

Neither of us sleep well that night, though not because of the *Fawlty Towers* enigma. I blame the heat and too many drinks at the hotel bar. But the following morning – our last in Torquay – a trio of late-middle-aged women, who resemble an ageing girl group, tell us it's the work of the supernatural.

'This hotel's haunted, I know it,' says one.

'Last night I felt the presence of my late mother,' says another.

'Are you mediums yourselves?' I ask them.

'No,' says the third one, 'but if you find one here let us know.'

It turns out they're veterans of Torquay's annual spiritualism festival. They tell me it's held in the Riviera Hotel every January.

We pack, check out and drive to the Bygones Museum. It's a highly detailed paste-up of a Victorian street. Modern-built rooms and wax mannequins are interspersed with period artefacts. A newsboy clutches an original copy of the London *Times* while a recorded actor's voice yells, 'Relief of Mafeking! Read all about it!' A squire with a greasy gerbil moustache reclines on a gout stool in his parlour. There's an apothecary and pub and bakery and tobacconist. They all contain gollies of differing frames and scales. The disturbing possibility comes to me that the management has deliberately sought them out and positioned them prominently around the place. The grocer's store is a nasty reminder that white supremacism was once a lucrative sales tactic. The centrepiece is a large advert for Robinson's jam featuring the com-

pany's golly mascot – abolished only in 2002. As late as the 1980s, kids would collect the stickers from the jars and send them off in exchange for a cute and furry little racist doll. Elsewhere in the mock shop is a Camp Coffee logo depicting a Sikh waiting obediently on a Highlander colonial soldier.

In Bygone's gift shop I conduct a social experiment on the old couple who run it. Mustering my best poker-face I ask, 'Is it possible to buy a golly?'

The couple's mouths flatline in worry. 'We used to sell them a while back,' says the woman, 'but people on the internet started giving us grief about it. There's no sense of humour these days.' She makes eye contact with me and lifts her eyebrows oh so slightly, as if signalling to me in code. 'Such a shame, don't you think?'

I make a non-committal noise at the back of my throat. I'm offended that she'd think I'd agree with her about some gilded Age of Prejudice. She must have looked me up and down and made a silent judgement based on my dress, accent, age, gender perhaps and certainly my ethnicity. Surely if a person of colour had asked her the same question – which would be a pretty weird thing to do in the first place – she'd have given a different reply. Or maybe she's self-deceiving enough to think that they wouldn't be offended by it either.

A jollier final impression of

Torquay is provided by Barracoon over the road. It's the most sophisticated model village that I've been to, with soundtracks, moving parts and a modern artist's instinct for the playful and satirical. There are scaled-down scenes referencing Eastenders and a hodge-podge of genuine and faux product placement. I prefer the mini supermarket called 'Litl' and coffee shop named 'Costalot' to trucks with 'British Petroleum' on them, which seems unethical. You'd think that seaside town-dwellers would be more concerned about what fossil fuels are doing to their environment.

While Barracoon provided some relief, Louis and I depart Torquay with ghosts, conspiracy theories, local icons (that weren't really) and Little England bigotry on our minds.

Don't Mock an Absence
Weston-super-Mare

In late summer 2015, the artist Banksy curated Dismaland, a happening in Weston-super-Mare that tried to lampoon the dowdy commercialism of seaside entertainment. A toy helicopter had been crashed head-first into a mini golf course already defaced by oil drum halves. A dark-stained fairy-tale palace looked on the cusp of collapse, shored up by rusty scaffolding and jagged teeth of corrugated iron inscribed with Banksyesque sentiments like UN-FUCK THE SYSTEM.

Some critics slammed Dismaland for its shortage of artistic invention and confusion of irony with sarcasm. A parody of a parody – or at least of something that never took itself seriously in the first place – doesn't always work. Few impersonations of or jokes about Donald Trump could scarcely be more absurd than Donald Trump. The same goes for Boris Johnson and Jacob Rees-Mogg. Long before Banksy's hidden hand started to pull the strings of contemporary art, seaside towns were a carnivalesque 'underbelly' poking fun at the English values of 'progress, respectability and modernity', as the historian Tony Bennett wrote. Bansky today could only dream of the infamy the seaside postcard designer Donald McGill gained from his obscenity bust back in 1954. Police seized twenty-four of his sauciest cartoons, which of course today seem tamer than a team of tranquilised tabby cats. A chubby-cheeked guy holding a colossal length of rock between his knees is captioned with 'A stick of rock, cock?' A voluptuous woman in only a pink bra and pink lace-top stockings sits on a bed gawking at a sign that says, 'Be prepared for the master cometh.' What's objectionable today about McGill's shtick is his misogyny and keenness to body-shame. The butts of his jokes are often enough the butts of rotund mothers-in-law or slender coquettes. In that regard Banksy's up-punching humour is at least a step forward.

But maybe Dismaland wasn't parodic enough. Several of its supposedly avant-garde installations would simply be called amusements in a genuine resort. Dismaland's Grim Reaper driving a bumper car was lauded as hilariously original by folks perhaps too posh to have been to any real funfairs themselves. I'm sure I've seen Death on a dodgem during a childhood trip to some pier or other at Halloween

time. The young Banksy might have encountered it too and forgot to give credit where due. Dismaland's staff were instructed to scowl rather than to smile at the public, but those who toil in arcades called Sunshine Pavilion and Stardust City don't need to be told to look pissed off. And go to any of the seaside towns mentioned in this book and you'll find a real eccentric performing the same role as the actor Banksy hired to wear a suit of tessellated union flags and pilot a mobility scooter with a scrawled sign reading 'save the pier while it's still here.'

Walking around Weston's Alexandra Parade area several years after Dismaland closed, the gap between the send-up and the thing being sent-up is distressingly tight. Besides, it feels wrong to even speak of comedy when social conditions are the opposite of funny. You know a town centre's in trouble when even its kebab shops are boarded up. Straits must be dire if there's no demand for a four-quid meal let alone the same amount for a drink, as pubs and nightclubs here now have peeling walls and blacked-out windows. At an earlier stage of belt-tightening, pricier activities like weddings were squeezed out, as the long-vacant bridal shop illustrates. These ghost streets have risen from the long-range demise of tourism in Weston, and shorter-term blows from Covid and soaring prices. There's never an equal distribution of

the pain. Catering to a flusher crowd, the Conservative Club and Royal Air Forces Association are in rude health.

While I could be guilty of removing red-eye and adding warmer filters to my mental pictures of Weston, it was in much better touch when I was last here in 2012. Hitting the beach with my then-partner and her 7-year-old daughter, we enjoyed the revivals of old pleasures – the donkey rides, rubber dinghies for hire and a Punch and Judy show cleaned up for 21st century mores. But Weston would literally lose its shine when the tide went out and revealed an expanse of mud – a result of the beach's proximity to the gravelly Bristol Channel and Severn Estuary. This can be a health hazard. Over one sweltering weekend in July 2021, coastguards salvaged over fifty people – including a twelve-year-old boy – who'd got stranded off 'Weston-super-Mud', as it's nicknamed. The coastguards put it down to post-lockdown euphoria. Like birds suddenly released from a cage, after being cooped up for so long people had the impulse to walk, run or swim further than ever.

This afternoon is calmer. It's an overcast weekday, after all. Louis and I pass a multi-ethnic smattering of families, one of Muslim women in hijabs and face masks, another comprising three generations of African men. Indeed, we see more people of colour in our first half-hour in Weston

than we did in 72 hours in Torquay. But there are also sunburned boomers in vests and sandals, and topless teens – guys not girls, of course – with the forward-combed buzzcuts popularised by the vintage violence drama *Peaky Blinders*, or *Brumwalk Empire* as I like to call it. Sometimes we catch them smiling wryly at us. They know they're not gangsters, we know that they know. And they know that we know that they know.

There's an absence of facilities too – another Covid hangover? – though the signage says otherwise. A billboard points to donkey rides that aren't there. Same for the bouncy castle. There's nothing Victorian about the Victorian Café, apart from it may have been closed for 150 years. The Sovereign Shopping Centre and Sandringham Gift Shop sound royal while not looking it. The York Hotel has probably needed a PR makeover since the office it was named after was dragged into the sewers by Prince Andrew.

The clouds thicken around the sun and spit down at us. Such conditions are never flattering to a town, so I'm willing to believe that, when the light's better, Weston Pier's threatening grey turrets look less like the Axis Chemical Factory from the Batman films and comics. I love the Axis Chemical Factory and so wouldn't be bothered if the pier bespoke it in all weathers, but I suspect I might be in the minority on

that one. It doesn't seem to have kept the cheery sunbathers and swimmers away down on the cocoa-powdery sand. Should I warn them that the consistency turns to mousse the further out they go? I'll let the signs do that.

The rain comes harder and faster. We quicken our pace through an elegant square – fountain out of action – and orbit a disused, litter-strewn car park daubed with graffiti that says BIG UP ISAMBARD BRUNEL. Brunel was the engineer who built so much in the southwest. Next door is the lot where we're parked. I notice a more formal announcement, perhaps Council-sponsored: WHAT ARE YOUR WISHES FOR WESTON? As an outsider who nonetheless gained an affection for the southwest while living in nearby Bristol, I wish the best for Weston. A good start would be restoring battered Birnbeck Pier, out of order and shrouded in barbed wire since 1979, but state-of-the-art in the 1860s. The only Grade II listed pier left in Britain, its dynamic, multi-directional walkways spidering across Birnbeck Island and mainland Weston would be a hard act to parody.

THE SOUTH
I Have Seen the Future of Seaside Towns
Bournemouth

I arrive in Bournemouth as certain English cultural stars are aligning. It's the year's first heatwave and England are playing their first game in a major football tournament – two events that typically cause English people to over-imbibe and do stupid things. When you add the significant loosening of Covid restrictions to that cocktail – and cocktail is the right metaphor, I think – people are likely to do even stupider things.

I am not above doing stupid things myself. The moment I step off the train, I search for a pub where I can watch the match and get told by every single bouncer in Bournemouth that their respective venues are fully booked. In between these venues, I dodge past pavement-filling phalanxes of bullet-headed boys with undercuts, hair left on top slicked back, war hero-style. A variation on the *Peaky Blinders* theme we saw in Weston. Half are cloaked in

George crosses. One drops a crate of premium lager to a chorus of 'Oi oiiiii-ii!' When I was their age, I avoided lads like that as they'd often shout 'freak' – or more creatively – 'Roswell' at me because I belonged to a rival subculture. We wore army surplus jackets and eyeliner rather than sportswear and mid-priced aftershave. Now, thankfully, I'm old, fat and grey enough not to draw their heat.

I call Louis – currently en route from the West Country – to say I'll watch the game at our hotel. As an American, he couldn't care less about football and will meet me later. The Royal Bath Hotel used to be the chic hangout of Oscar Wilde and the revered

actors Sarah Bernhardt and Sir Henry Irving... but that was 130 years ago. Where once there were crystal chandeliers and exquisite repartee there are now threadbare, mould-green settees and the rising and falling cicada-like buzz of the crowd coming from two infuriatingly small TVs showing England v Croatia. One family, whose matriarch has a spindly, downturned nose like a cigarette that needs to be tapped for ash, have selfishly pushed their chairs in so close to one screen that no one else in the lobby can see it. Hubby looks like someone trying unconvincingly to disguise himself as someone else. The all-too-brittle bouffant looks as fake as the tan and the moustache, which dips

low to the right either because (a) it really is false and hasn't been glued on properly or (b) it's real and the man's face is oddly asymmetrical. Another old-timer with burst blood vessels on his face like a spray of buckshot gambols from the bar, quivering hands round a bottle of rosé.

'It's a good feeling to hear the national anthem again,' says the commentator before proudly pointing out that, in this European football tournament, all of England's matches will be played in London. 'Can we do it again all these years after 1966?' he adds. Such patriotic patter sounds more desperate than usual, a papering over the cracks of post-Brexit economic woes and just after a lockdown during which politicians and elements of the media urged national unity as a response to Covid – instead of a proper response that might have saved thousands of lives.

At half-time with Ingerland 1-0 up and spirits high, a sparklingly bald fellow flops down next to me. 'Who score?' he asks in an Eastern European accent. Perhaps as an expression of nationalistic zeal there's a contest amongst those sitting around me to tell him first. 'Sterling! Sterling! Sterling!' they grunt in quick succession.

I ask the man if he lives in Bournemouth.

'No, London. But I visit here for many year. Now, no good.' He points to the scraggy *fleur-de-lys* carpet that's tainted by the odd crisp, twig and bottle cap. 'Not so clean now. Me and wife want to use spa this year but spa not open yet. And you buy pint here and they not fill it up to top of glass, so not pint really.'

Even so, he says he loves Bournemouth Beach as there's nothing like it in London. Nor is there in Cracow, where he's from originally. His dream

is to live on the beach one day. He feels the pull of the deep blue because, as a floorer, he's spent much of his working life inland and indoors in dry, hot, tight spaces.

When the second half of the match begins, he tells me he dislikes the number of foreigners now playing for English clubs. 'Each team should have only player born near that team.' He's lucky there isn't the same policy towards, say, Polish skilled labourers who want to come to London.

'How is Poland these days?' I ask.

'Most corrupt country in world. Nurse not give injection to patient unless nurse take bribe first.'

When I reply that there's corruption all over the world – Britain definitely included – he glares at me like I've just got naked. 'Not like Poland,' he insists.

The rosé-bibber from earlier lurches up to us and grips the headrest of the Pole's armchair. 'Whassa score then?' he rasps, even though the score is right in front of his eyes on the TV screen.

'1-0,' I inform him.

'We should be doing better, shouldn't we?'

'But Croatia good,' says the Pole.

'Oh,' sighs Rosé-Bibber. Clearly, he knows even less about modern football

than I do. He lurches off.

'There's still time for things to go pear-shaped,' I warn with the fatalism of the England fan, justified by an epic record of errors such as star players getting sent off for kicking an opponent rather than the ball.

The Pole puts it more charitably: 'Over years England have lot of unluckiness.'

I succumb to another football cliché when I accidentally shout 'You idiot!' after Sterling fluffs a chance from the edge of the box. I've forgotten that I'm not in a rowdy pub and earn evil eyes from the soporific persons around me. The retirement home vibe extends to the garden where more old folks ease themselves off and onto sunbeds on the stripey lawn.

Bournemouth Beach is the exact opposite: young, vibrant, multiethnic, multicultural. It's as if the thousand feet-long pier is a pipeline inhaling something of the diversity of the world beyond Dorset. It's maniacally crowded. Bodies of all shapes and shades are laid out in close proximity like dominoes. No wonder there was a Covid super-spread here last summer. Orthodox Jewish boys lob an American football about. Lithe Mediterranean girlfriends zoom down the zipline one-by-one, faces taut with horror and joy. Conspicuous amongst these fun-lovers are quieter, sterner-looking youths. Their designer shades and high-end

stereo kit could mean they're either the children of hedge-fund managers or they've got prematurely rich from crime.

I pause to watch a South Asian man, belly tumbling over Bermudas, wading solo out to sea, filming himself on his phone. He's just one of many clutching an electronic device wince-makingly close to the water. On the pier, a dozen Filipinas snap each other pouting and making peace signs. Behind them, trunked and turbaned Sikh lads record a rubber dinghy overflowing with their cheering friends as it drifts between the stilts and through the shadows under the pier. Everything is a performance to be documented, stored, shared – truly a 21st century seaside experience.

This isn't the only of Bournemouth's qualities to feel contemporary. The Internet of Things is closer to being realised here than it is in Torquay

or Weston, with free Wifi available from every nook of the pier and at many of the businesses around it. Another progressive feature is the electric barbecues laid out for public use – although who knows what state they'll be in when this party's over. Even the ice cream has evolved beyond the primitive Mr Whippy into advanced new species like lotus caramelised biscoff. One shop though, is surely not cool enough for this crowd, but I remark on it purely because I haven't seen anything quite like it in other resorts. Belying its name, Urban Beach sells New Age tat from pagan amulets to tarot card tapestry flags, whatever the hell they are.

The air is layered with myriad smoke – incense, barbecued meat, exhaust fumes from car-clogged Bath Road, weed, tobacco, perhaps other flammable drugs. A sonic collage has been made from every human vocalisation – whoops to whines, shrieks to sighs, yips to yawns. Somewhere in the mix, Afrobeat, grime, drum 'n' bass and Turkish pop blast from amped-up iPhones.

I bump into a Frisbee-eared bloke pointing his phone camera at the underside of the pier. Hi-vis-vested security guards hurtle down there. 'Let's see what's what,' says the man in a conspiratorial Scottish accent. The skirmish is

over before we arrive. The guards are telling off a bunch of lads who are now bowing their heads or crossing their arms defensively.

'Really changed since I lived here ten years ago,' sighs the Scotsman. 'Gangs are big now. Stabbings in the park, that kinda thing.'

'Do they mostly come from London?' I ask.

'Aye. The M3 was bloody rammed this morning.'

I meet Louis by a couple of half-rhyming signs. They seem naive given the mess there will be come sudown.

IF IT DIDN'T COME FROM YOU, DON'T FLUSH IT DOWN THE LOO SHOW YOUR LOVE FOR THE BEACH AND HELP CREATE A LITTER-FREE COAST AND SEA

Seeing how busy the beach is, we're not surprised to find back at the hotel a young couple crestfallen at being turned away. 'All 140 of our rooms are booked out,' says the hang-dog clerk. We go and eat in the Royal Bath's own restaurant named Oscar's after Mr Wilde. It's a mistake. The price of spending an hour in a room that the great author once sashayed through is mediocre, pre-Gourmet England cuisine. Insipid gravy, latex turkey – or is it chicken, we have no idea – and veg boiled for so long they may have been sentenced to a Tudor execution. Our fellow diners are in better shape than I

despite being at least thirty years older, but that might be due to eating minimal amounts of garbage like this all their lives. I recall the Rolling Stones guitarist Keith Richards saying that being kept underfed as a kid had helped keep him stay slim in later life. Well, that and the heroin, I guess. The saving grace of

Oscar's – and the reason we don't go to bed on an empty stomach – is the rhubarb crumble. It's rich, crunchy and perfectly pitched between sweet and sharp. Almost worth the £14.50 alone. One thing pre-Gourmet England did well was puddings.

To find the whole of Bourne-

mouth's restaurant scene guilty based on the crimes of Oscar's would be a good old-fashioned British miscarriage of justice. Aside from the rotten egg that is Oscar's – and I'd fully expect that item to be on their breakfast menu – the basket is stupendous, with Charminster Road as manifoldly

scrumptious as anywhere in central London. Persian, Lebanese, Nigerian, South African, Korean, Indian, Chinese, Thai... all within a mile or so. Near-by Zephyr is a cool rock bar, low-lit, decorated with portraits of Lemmy and Iggy Pop, and well-stocked with foreign beers. The most pretentious drink-and-eatery we come across – which would therefore be at home in the most pretentious districts of London, New York or Tokyo – is done out in black-ink graffiti and staffed by an androgynous cyberpunk serving exorbitant pot noodles.

Later, at a bar nearer the seafront that purports to be 1990s-themed but isn't aside from serving bottles of Hooch (remember that anyone over thirty-five?), a teen with dark brushy hair asks Louis if he will draw him in return for a round of beers. While Louis labours, the teenager tells me the government has paid him to go on holiday in Bournemouth. 'I'm from St Ives,' he says, 'where the G7 conference is on.'

Once I've studied my mental image of Biden, Modi and Xi Xinping sharing a cream tea in a sleepy Cornish town, I ask him why he had to leave.

'Security. Me flat's near the venue. Apparently, Boris has been swimming in the sea right outside me window. They offered me neighbour 1200 quid for a sniper to sit on his roof. They say the Queen gave permission to set

up these temporary buildings, also for security.'

It all strikes me as rather feudal – the barons bribing the peasants off their land. How does he feel about it?

'It's nice to have a free holiday and that, but you got all these people coming to St Ives and none of their money's going to businesses there apart from the touristy places. And most of the area's been closed off. Residents can't even walk around there. It's mad.'

The lad is thrilled at Louis' depiction of him and says he'll hang it in his local pub. 'By the time you come to St Ives, mate, you'll be a hero,' he promises. 'Just don't come till this stupid conference is over.'

Louis and I get our own taste of aloof authoritarianism in our second hotel in Bournemouth. While we're sympathetic to the knocks taken by the hospitality sector lately, in this particular establishment Covid is a lame excuse for everything being a bit crap. I glean this from a tense exchange with the receptionist. His fussy mien is reflected by his severely side-parted hair and nasally, undulating voice.

'What time's breakfast?' I ask.

'Sorry sir, since Covid we've not served breakfast or any other meal for that matter.'

'But I thought I saw a restaurant-'

'It's closed.'

That's weird, I say to myself. Our

last hotel managed to feed its guests, though not with food worth eating.

'Do you have an ironing board I could borrow?'

'We do, but we don't let it out of the utility room, so you'd have to bring your clothes there.'

'Why's that?'

'Covid precaution, sir. We're minimising movement around the hotel.'

With policies like this, they'll be minimising any chance of being solvent in six months. 'It's sweltering,' I say, 'and I can't turn on the air-conditioning.'

'We disconnected all the units, sir.'

'Covid again?'

'No, a few years ago the chain we belong to decided it wasn't cost-effective.'

'Do you have a fan?'

'Usually, sir, but they're all out on loan to other guests. Do hope you understand.'

My room's other shortcomings also pre-date the pandemic. There's less than the width of a shoe between the end of the bed and the cramped-together desk, TV and cupboard. Whereas in other hotels they leave plastic packs of teabags and biscuits by the cup and saucer, here there's only one teabag – not in a plastic pack – and no sign of any biscuits. I try and look on the bright side – no plastic is eco-friendlier and I should probably lay off the biscuits for health reasons. The complimenta-ry soap and bottle of shampoo are so small they'd barely clean a Borrower.

Whatever these discomforts, the next morning's another stunner. We set out for Sandbanks, a skinny peninsula four miles west of Bournemouth. It hosts some of the priciest property in the country. Celebrities, especially ones who have done well out of football, own multimillion-pound holiday homes there. This is to the chagrin of permanent residents, we learned from an off-duty tour guide at breakfast, because it entices noisy, drunken tourists the moment the weather turns nice.

It's a neat touch that all public buses round here are designed like tour buses, with open-top upper decks. The views from our bus bolsters my sense that Bournemouth is a class act. The architecture's a tasteful montage of Art Deco arches, well-buttressed Gothic churches, smart condominiums done out in the glossy, rectangular, International style, other contemporary houses with cantilevered balconies and Japanese minimalist lines. Living in a city with few trees, I appreciate Bournemouth's bonanza of pines, oaks, cypresses and palms. Of course, money is the main reason why all this is feasible in Bournemouth but not in other seaside towns. But all the same it's good to look at as you cruise about on a marvellous July afternoon.

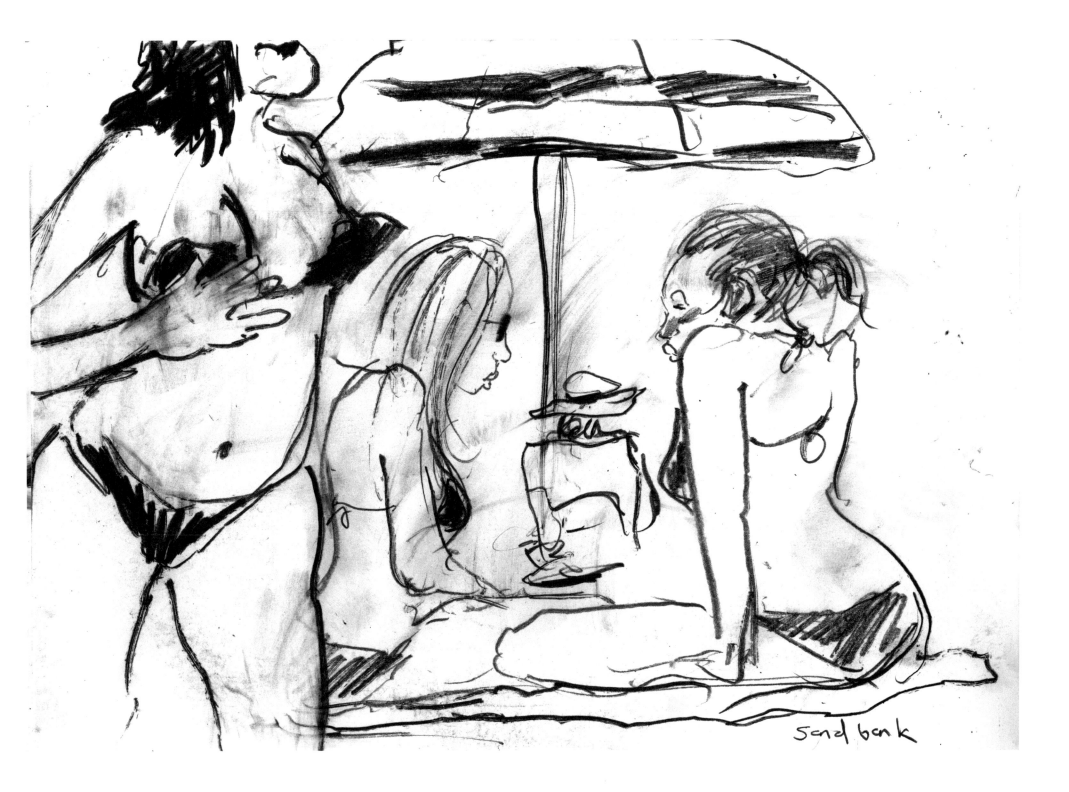

East vs West
Sandbanks and Boscombe

Although Sandbanks Beach isn't a private beach as such, it's demarcated by a row of sandwich boards saying no barbecues after 6pm and no dogs allowed between May and September. Beyond this impromptu border is a beach office and a highbrow fish-and-chips restaurant that sells nothing under £10. I guess this gives Sandbanks an air of separateness – if not exclusivity – that might please the snobbish.

It's as rammed as Bournemouth Beach was yesterday – and as performative. In the shallows, a dad crouches to photograph his four toddlers who strike various poses from body-builder clenches to arms outstretched like aircraft wings. It could be an avant-garde dance class. Then Dad takes more snaps of Mum and Aunties gripping the kids to their chests. Behind them is proof of our other national obsession. A student-aged guy squats as the waves splash over him and his Jack Russell, whom he periodically lets out on its lead and then draws back in for a cuddle.

Watching armies of kids charging full-pelt into the sea reminds me of Tommies going over the top in World War I. It's an odd analogy, I know, but *I am* odd. By contrast, the older swimmers are much slower into the water, gradually adjusting to its coldness.

I'm the same. As an overweight, middle-aged bloke whose maternal grandad died of a heart attack around the age that I am now, I shouldn't risk needless shocks.

Churning up the sea like convicts breaking rocks, jet skis form a chaotic cordon around the paddlers and swimmers. As with motorbiking, are power-trippers and attention-seekers drawn to this pursuit? 'Look at me, I can make lots of noise and hurt you if you come near.'

Half an hour later, direct hostility is on show. High-pitched and garbled shouting turns everyone's heads to a circle of teenage girls in swimming costumes. The circle breaks to reveal a red-haired wretch, hands cupping nose, blood dripping onto chin. How many of the super-rich are looking down on this and fretting about the prices of their clifftop mansions?

To relieve the tension, we play crazy golf. I like this game because it's a spoof of a game I dislike. Proper golf seems to consist of Trumpesque businessmen strutting about in silly trousers acting like they own half the countryside – which often they do. But with crazy golf there's no pomposity. Each hole is based on some gimmick like a scale model yacht or loop-the-loop Scalextric track. Sandbanks' course spills fetchingly across some steppes that lead down to a way trendier attraction: an authentic Finnish

wood-fired saltwater sauna with LED lighting, Douglas fir floorboards and British sheep's wool insulation. From the outside it looks like a garden shed. According to its slick website, this joint is so cool it doesn't sell tickets, it offers *experiences*. But we can't even have one of those because the Saltwater Sauna – to give its formal title – is shut for the foreseeable future.

Along the seafront back to Bournemouth are overflowing recycling bins, bacon bap kiosks and uniform beach huts like suburban bungalows. If it wasn't for the golden beach to our left this could be Anywheresville, Inland England. Those stranded in the no man's land between Sandbanks and Bournemouth, in places named Canford Cliffs and Alum Chine, are whiter, older and poorer than their counterparts in those richer resorts. A one-armed, aubergine-shaped woman jogger. A council worker with a Johnsonian tangle of blonde hair sweeping dog shit, roll-up sagging from his mouth. A Trilby on a mobility scooter pulling over every ten yards to stare out to sea with moist, melancholy eyes. A pensioner overdressed for twenty-four-degree heat in a cap, fleece and blazer all made from dense wool.

There's a Californian aesthetic to Branksome Beach's outdoor gym called, inventively, "Who Dares Gyms" and a watersports school shielded by paddles dug into the sand. We almost collide

with a flabby pubescent skateboarder. A sign asserting that this is the COAST WITH THE MOST is as bereft of modesty as any claim that's ever been made for California by a Californian.

Much like the old Cold War divide, west of Bournemouth is better-off than east of it. Thirty minutes' walk in the latter direction is the faded monochrome Boscombe Pier. The few people on it look so unhappy that they may soon jump off. There's nothing to do here than have a drink in the Harvester pub and then piss it out in the adjacent public toilet. A joint called Pier View is advertised as a 'venue for hire', but it looks to have been shut since Little

and Large last crowdsurfed and injected speedballs round these parts.

The beach throng is geriatric, mostly women. Blonde-white hair on scowls pivoting on reddening bodies that twist and turn in deck chairs – that masochistic English way of sunbathing. The mood's different outside a tea shop up on Boscombe Promenade. A confetti-haired woman hoots insanely as if she's having a clotted cream-induced orgasm. As unsettling is a mural of a little boy with gaping eyes, one palm pressed against the glass of a claw grab arcade machine, a heap of furry toys within. I'm reminded of those 'creepypasta' internet memes

that transform ordinary things – food, clowns, dolls, cartoons – into sinister imagery.

Outside Reefride Stores we catch a gobbet of talk between two nurses that must speak for billions: 'It's a miracle we didn't kill each other over lockdown'. In the shop I buy a postcard-sized painting of a tropical utopia of dolphins diving and waves barrelling around a palm-lined desert island. Inconceivably, the title of the piece is 'Boscombe'. I ask the young clerk where the dolphins are.

'Not much going on in Boscombe,' she smiles. She points to where we've just walked from. 'It's nicer that way in Bournemouth. Then even nicer over in Sandbanks.'

'Was it busy here after the football?'

'There was a fight after the football.' She rolls her eyes. 'Boys of course.'

That's three acts of violence – two involving lads – in 48 hours that Louis and I have either seen first-hand or heard about.

Sea Road leads us inland to Boscombe town and it's Bournemouth-plush. San Remo Towers is a stately block of Hispanic-Californian flats with taupe brickwork and voluptuous balconies. Revealing more about local spending power is a gastropub and a yuppie surf shop flogging backpacks for £80 that look as though they'd dis-

Boscombe beach

integrate in a day.

Sea Road pedestrianises into a classic English working-class town centre. The locally peculiar rubs shoulders with the multinational. The South West Regional Assessment Centre and Body Snatchers Boxing Gym are round the corner from KFC and McDonald's. There are kebab grills, greasy spoons, vape shops, bookies, a pizzeria in the colours of the Italian flag. Bosc Vegas is the name of the most rundown of the night-windowed cornershops hawking cut-price firewater. The Royal Arcade, noted for its Victorian intricacy, is shrouded in scaffolding today. Boscombe's only other uncommon feature is the Tropical Fish and Reptile Centre where you can buy a male green iguana for £375. Not many of those for sale on high streets these days.

It's not hard to imagine this part of town hosting sixty drug rehabilitation services amid a population of 21,000 – the highest per capita in England and Wales. The thirty-five deaths from overdoses in 2018 also broke national records. But we can only imagine it, for after an hour here we find no evidence of what the tabloid papers have called 'Trainspotting-on-Sea'. Well, that is, apart from a strung-out fellow with a shell-suit blazer tied round his waist, begging passersby for the price of a

train fare to nowhere. I doubt you'd see something like this in Bournemouth, the imperative being to keep social catastrophes out of tourists' sight. After all, the guilty bargain of gentility is that it's scored at the expense of somewhere else, nearby, being not very genteel at all.

Beside the Sea Signs
Southbourne, Hengistbury Head and Mudeford

Something you find at the English seaside that you won't on foreign coasts are benches with memorial plaques on them. While I could be wrong, I've never seen public seating in Goa or Grand-Bassam with text to this effect: 'Dear old Alfie Belcher (1914-1995), he loved to eat cockles here with a knotted handkerchief on his head. Love sister Ethel and daughter Marjorie x x x'. Along the cliffs going east from Boscombe are plaques accompanied by flowers, cuddly toys and other votives to the dead. Such ritualism tells us something about a culture's priorities. The messages refer to the significance of the seaside to ordinary people: 'Bernie Kitson – I must go down to the sea today (1950-2021); 'Tony (1924-2010) and Winnie (1919-2014) loved the bay', and so on. An optimism – and naivety? – is implied by the medium for these messages: outdoor furniture rendered unusable for long periods by poor weather. But there's something reverent about the benches facing the sea. When Bernie and Tony and Winnie stared into the cobalt vastness did they have the sublime sensation that, like a deity, the ocean was infinitely mightier than they were – or would ever be?

Less lofty sentiments have been daubed alongside the plaques on Southbourne's benches. In hysterical, garish, all-capitals Tippex: SAVE OUR CHILDREN FROM THIS EXPERIMENTAL VACCINE - THE CLOT SHOT. Whatever your views on jabs, it seems at the very least poor optics to spray this propaganda on these monuments to those whose lives were probably either saved or extended by mass-vaccination programmes throughout the 20th century.

We plod on amid spitty rain like a garden sprinkler on a misty setting. Saner signs – DANGER - KEEP OFF CLIFF – speak to another social crisis hitting our shoreline hard. In 2017-20, the number of Dorset men who took their own lives increased by 5% compared to the previous three years. Scarborough, Clacton and Blackpool, which Louis and I will visit soon, have some of the highest suicide rates in England. Many of the victims faced financial adversity – in 2019, more bankruptcies were declared in Scarborough than anywhere else in England.

Beside Overcliff Drive roundabout is a petite but well-appointed community garden with flourishing bushes, homemade bird feeders and a construct that resembles a wicker man. The hand-scrawled pleas on its fence are dispatches from a culture war that's older and even more divisive than vaccination – the struggle of commoners against the wolfish appetites of property and capital.

NO FLATS HERE
SAVE OUR GREEN SPACE
SAVE SOUTHBOURNE CROSS ROADS

On the footpath down the precipice are words in different fonts snipped from newspapers and rearranged into a document whose allusion to either ransom notes or the Sex Pistols will be lost on younger readers:

COUNCIL SCANDAL OF PARKING SELL OFF
FOR RICH PICKINGS
STAND AND FIGHT TO STOP PUBLIC LAND SELL OFF
OBJECT ONLINE NOW

As if to prove these activists' point, we find a whole stretch of Overcliff Drive phosphorescent with new-build luxury flats. Billboards for a pilates studio and a Bistro on the Beach are further markers of new money. Sometimes seaside signs signify nothing. This is true of Hengistbury Head, a moody promontory rippling with velvety heath that won't be built on because it's a habitat for kestrels to nightjars, stag beetles to peacock butterflies, badgers to adders. There are some vivid artists' impressions of these creatures on the signs that also reveal their Latin names and summarise their lifestyles. The only problem is, we don't see any real creatures apart from seagulls – and you don't need to go to a national park for those. Mind you, I'm glad I didn't meet an adder.

The final sign of the day is ambiguous and disturbing. We round Hengistbury and enter Mudeford's range of reed-topped dunes that separate the smudgy blue waters of Christchurch Bay and a column of clapboard beach huts. These huts are the most expensive in Britain, some worth more than £300,000 apiece. A privilege of owning one is that you can sleep in it overnight – and you can't do that in its bog-standard counterparts anywhere else in the UK. Then again, I wonder who would bother to police this.

We sit for a sip of water at a wooden table and chairs – the least the local authorities can lay on given the amount of council tax they must reap from these big-shot bungalows. Hold on, do you have to pay council tax on a £300,000 beach hut? I have no idea and I now hate myself for even asking such a bourgeois question. I notice that someone has placed a sticker onto one of the table legs that seems madder than a one-inch airport: YOU DO NOT REQUIRE ANYBODY'S PERMISSION TO BREATHE FREELY – TAKE OFF THE MUZZLE.

And why make this command in a spacious, outdoor environment where masks are unlikely to be worn anyway? Is it instead a metaphor for free speech or some other right that's being eroded? Code for a conspiracy as per the earlier swipes against property developers? We glance about for clues.

Seems congenial enough here, but then what do we really know as day-trippers, as outsiders without an understanding of these signs beside the seaside and what they may mean to a community, if anything much?

THE EAST
A Couple of Clactons
Clacton-on-Sea

On the train to Essex, I realise I know little about Essex. And that little is scrappy and second-hand. Growing up in the 1990s, I recall the 'Essex Man' media stereotype. He'd flourished, so this crude narrative went, under Thatcher by dragging himself out of the working class on the spoiler of a second-hand car. Dodgy motors – along with watches, jewellery, video recorders and discount clothing – were the sources of the entrepreneurial Essex Man's income, which he spent on tasteless nouveau riche trappings like mock Tudor houses, gaudy shirts and white stilettos for his trophy wife ('Essex Girl' was the complementary – though not complimentary – female version). Both boilerplates must have been dreamed up by middle-class snobs, for the claim was that Essex Man and Essex Girl had grown up in the sooty, shabby East End of London before moving further east to cleaner, brighter coastal resorts like Clacton-on-Sea, where I was headed now.

Sometimes Essex Man fled to southern Shangri-Las like Hayling Island, where I grew up. One case – although the only Essex Man cliché he observed was voting Tory – was the father of my childhood best friend Pete

Taylor, who passed far too young in 2019. Pete dreaded having to visit his relatives in Essex during the school holidays and took revenge by co-writing with me a comedy screenplay that posited the county as a hub of hardboiled crime. The script was titled *Chelmsford Confidential*, a reference to *LA Confidential*, the neo-noir film popular at the time. Not a great pun, but we were only seventeen at the time. One of Pete's most memorable inventions was 'Clacton Contract Killers', which paired an image of English seaside kitsch with that of Tarantino-esque assassins. Pete also created a character called the Reverend Chingford W. Manslaughter – Church of England vicar by day, Glock-toting gangster by night. While we were working on the first draft, I recall saying that 'a Clacton' sounds like an insult, as in 'You're a right Clacton, you are'. The word's clumsy phonetics evoke stupidity or naïvety, like 'dimwit' or 'bumpkin'.

So now, having never been to Clacton, Chingford or Chelmsford, I can only mentally associate these places with my much-missed friendship with Pete, my first efforts at writing more than twenty years ago and, most curiously, a Chandleresque criminal demimonde. The real Clacton is a disappointment on that last count, though it's not without problems. These are evident from my 10-minute walk from train station to b&b. A topless guy

squats and shivers in a Co-op doorway. A rain mac-encased woman tows a trolley of shoes and tinned food, her tongue enlarged from some illness, looking like a macaroon clasped between her lips. Two puffer jackets share a spliff, one to the other, 'I've signed up to PIP but now Universal Credit are telling me I gotta find a job. What's all that about, eh?'

After dropping off my stuff at the b&b, I trudge along the coast towards Clacton Pier where I'm due to meet Louis. I pass an ad for a Jim Davidson gig and a bus shelter housing a Gandalfian beard on a mobility scooter also getting stoned. The backdrop to the coastal road is cheerier. Out to sea, a rainbow flares through the inky clouds above a graceful procession of wind turbines.

The pier itself is drabber and could be confused for an industrial road bridge if it wasn't for the ice cream cone-shaped helter-skelter, fake lighthouse, fake palm trees. A billboard boasts CLACTON PIER – NO. 1 NORTH SEA. But what's the competition? Oil rigs? The pier backs on, germanely enough, to Pier Avenue, belted by arcades and cheap eateries. I find Louis, who observes that the latticework bannister on the mezzanine floor of Charnallies Restaurant and Bar – the largest single building on the avenue – has a 19th-century New Orleans vibe. Behind us is the subtler Venetian

Bridge, built in 1914 as a facsimile of... the bridges you find in Venice presumably. Maybe seaside towns, located as they are at points where England interacts with the outside world via the ocean, import symbols from overseas to lend themselves some glamour and excitement. I don't think we've been to a coastal arcade yet that hasn't invoked Monte Carlo casinos, Aztec emperors, Egyptian pharaohs, plus all stripes of Americana, from the Wild West to Mississippi riverboat gambling. These may be the tips of conceptual icebergs that run deep into a popular unconscious formed when Britain was bossing Johnny Foreigner Land with crass assumptions about its mystery, exoticism and hidden riches.

Caught in the radioactively bright lights of arcades called Gameshow and Magic City are the leopardskin-spotted and the latex-legged and the Adidas-zipped and the pasty-faced. But we also spot mixed race couples, a Muslim family in trad garb and dapper young mums with dapper tots.

Not that any of this makes for friendliness. I ask some teens exiting a snooker hall what it's like.

'Nice,' mutters one of the girls, while the others pocket their hands and recoil from me.

'Is it still open?'

'Shut.'

I ask if there's anywhere else round here you can get a drink at 11pm.

'Naah.'

I try to bring the others into the conversation. 'You guys from round here then?'

'Near,' says the girl. Everyone else stays eye-uncontactable.

Later it comes to me that these kids might have thought it was, for a whole suite of reasons, a bit strange to chat with two tipsy old farts their dads' age.

We do manage to find a pub still open. According to not overly reliable TripAdvisor comments, the Moon and Starfish is the worst Wetherspoon's in the entire country – a laurel over which there must be fierce rivalry. Louis and I know immediately that we've been to much worse. It's boisterous but also more hospitable than the teenagers were. Blokes apologise in classic English style for no other reason than wanting to let you past them in the corridor. From the next table I eavesdrop on a Geordie saying, 'Aye, it's alright here, like' and a local responding, 'You're welcome any time, mate.'

When we hobble outside at 1 am, we're caught in a power ballad crossfire. From the right we're barraged by a karaoke version of 'Show Me Heaven' which, delivered by a flat, baritone voice through a distorted microphone, sounds like it's being sung by Pinhead the demon from the contemporaneous *Hellraiser* horror films. The no less diabolical 'I've Had the Time of My Life'

strafes us from the left, out of a nightclub with the Orwellian name 'Truth'.

The eighties theme stretches to the Clacton Pavilion. Louis and I go there next morning to find reboots of Pacman and Space Invaders machines, and a scalloped old dear on death's door playing a Tim Burton's *Batman* slot machine. While she must have been at least 124 when that film came out in 1989, Louis and I were kids then and it's depressing that, for total lack of new cultural ideas, the songs, films and games of our youth are now being lazily recycled – and heavily monetised – by the seaside fun industry in the same way as those phoney pharaohs. I'm not sure how good Maria McKee and Michael Keaton were the first time round, much less the second. But maybe they give parents of my generation a nos-

I'm just moderately cynical.

Ever ginger about where to sit, draw and make notes, Louis and I plump for Luca's Ice Cream Parlour. I soon realise it's attached to a kids' soft play area. My heartbeat hastens. In any sane world, a law-abiding middle-aged man who doesn't look too dodgy should be free to go in public where he pleases. But in the real world, plagued by paedophile paranoia, a law-abiding middle-aged man who looks a bit dodgy in a certain light can fall under suspicion for being around children if he isn't accompanied by a child of his own.

A waitress comes to our table. 'I'm afraid I'm going to have to ask you to leave,' she says firmly but respectfully. A fiery blush spreads over my face. Have we been barred for alleged noncery? Perhaps feeling bad about distressing me and/or now entertaining the possibility that Louis and I are a gay couple, she asks, 'Do you have children in the play area?'

'No.'

'This space is reserved for parents only.'

She smiles. I smile. Louis smiles. She smiles back. Then the thought flashes that perhaps we're all smiling too much, like we're creepy and she's placating us.

'Of course, of course, of course.' Louis and I both say that phrase a few too many times for comfort.

Rather than learning from our *faux pas*, we go and do something potentially even weirder than sitting near children: we play children's games amid loads of children. In our defence, we're professionally obliged to at least have a quick go on them – the games, that is. Like the model village, the coin drop machine captures in miniature something of the economics and geography of seaside towns. The metal cliffs are piled high with 2ps and 10ps, the odd few slipping over the edges like eroded shards of sandstone. The claw machines are as literal a manifestation of the phrase 'money-grabbing' as you'll find. However, they require more skill than simply dropping coins, as you guide with a joystick a sinister metal pincer – like the one replacing the hand of Tee Hee, the baddie from the James Bond film *Live and Let Die* – towards a poor innocent teddy bear. Never in my life having won a thing from these infuriating devices, this afternoon I finally do win something. When a furry, police tape-yellow Pacman toy tumbles out, I hold it aloft like a football captain showing off his new FA Cup. I'm sure that looked weirder still.

Do these slot machines and their hard-to-attain rewards typify the misplaced hope that many seaside townies have about luck smiling on them – winning the lottery, say, or marrying someone rich – and climbing out of their humdrum jams? In the Great Depression, punters who'd got

used to doing without the finer things were obsessed with the Clucking Hen contraption, which laid gaudy metal eggs in return for a penny. According to Kathryn Ferry, Britain was importing 5 million such eggs from Germany until World War II broke out and Hitler redeployed the manufacturers to making bombs and bullets instead.

Clacton Pavilion's size is matched by some of the games within it. The Xtreme Big One must be the Burj Khalifa of claw machines, at over ten feet tall and pillow-sized items of Spiderman merchandise – again literally – up for grabs. At the seaside images are not only constantly copied but adapted for different formats. These Spiderman prizes are by-products of a multinational racket that evolved from a humble sixties comic book. Less lucrative yet more eerie are the polyester doughnuts that line the shelves of a tin can shooting range... that stands opposite other stalls where you can buy real doughnuts. Other seaside foods are so iconic that they've been almost infinitely reproduced. And why not in an age when all kinds of other data are proliferating on a mind-blowing scale? I think back to our trips to the West Country and how it would be very easy to walk out of just one gift shop wearing a T-shirt depicting a Cornish pasty, a baseball cap depicting a Cornish pasty and two Cornish pasty-shaped slippers, with a Cornish pasty-shaped pencil case in

one hand and, least excitingly, an actual Cornish pasty in the other. At some dystopian rupture in our near future, will the hot, meat-filled snack that we know today as the Cornish pasty be eclipsed by innumerable replicas of it? Again, why not when you consider that, although dinosaurs died out 65 million years ago, they continue to appear in movies, theme parks and the highest echelons of the British government. Just as the Campaign for Real Ale was founded in the 1960s out of terror that traditional beer that tasted of something was being submerged under an avalanche of mass-produced pastiches of a beer that tasted of nothing (Watney's Red Barrel et al), perhaps there will soon be a Campaign for Real Cornish Pasties.

Such a campaign may already have started in a pub that we must negotiate to escape the pavilion. Before a deafening live band doing a lesser Britpop cover, families are scarfing meals that I thought had been extinct in this country since we realised, some time towards the end of the last century, that hot cuisine could be a touch more stimulating than triads of tinned legumes, cremated potatoes and shreds of low-grade flesh, whether served naked, battered or pastry-incarcerated. When I was bumming around as a young fool in Southeast Asia in the noughties, I met a French chef who'd catered for English tastes some time before this great

realisation. After sighing when I told him I was English – as French people will when you tell them you're English – he said that, while working in a Swiss hotel in the eighties, he'd been driven to distraction by tourists, mostly from London and Essex, ordering nothing but chicken and chips. He'd spent years perfecting his *blanquette de veau, crême brulée* and *béchamel* sauce recipes, only to be reduced to bunging prefab crap into a microwave.

On his 1933 tour of England – which took in bits of Essex – the playwright JB Priestley slammed the 'barbarism' of 'English cookery'. There was an exception to the rule: the 'venerated and idealized' steak, as he put it. 'When an ordinary English waiter mentions any other dish,' continued Priestley, 'he is a realist and his very tone of voice tells you what that dish really is – muck.' But the waiters here in Clacton, almost ninety years later, have no steak to offer, only mucky-looking chips, baked beans and pasties, pies or fish fingers. In the interest of balance, though, there's another restaurant inside the pavilion called Armstrong's which is excellent, as Louis and I find out that evening. The fresh, subtle and global menu rescues us back to the English culinary present.

Venturing beyond Pier Avenue we're faced with two contrasting Clactons.

1. Rough and Ready Clacton Northwest around the junction between Rosemary and Jackson Roads businesses play on the anxieties and profit from the weaknesses of the have-nots. Tattooists and manicurists supply that enduring demand to look good next to everyone else. In the

social media age, the contest has gone gladiatorial. If you're hard-up enough to steal things you can fence them, no questions asked, at the neo-pawn shop Cex (pronounced 'sex'). For me there's nothing less suggestive of love-making than a hooky food mixer, but maybe I'm just prudish. The already cash-strapped will have to tighten that strap after a visit to the bookie's, the payday loan shark or Argos (tempting folks into personal debt since 1972). Greggs and McDonald's are a cheap means to a short-term salt 'n' sugar hit, but in the longer term they've contributed to Clacton being named in a recent

government investigation as one of the unhealthiest coastal populations in the country. Further opportunities to slash your life expectancy are provided by old-fashioned tobacconists that these days must be as endangered as their patrons.

Rough and Ready Clacton's axis is the Rajul News and Booze cornershop. Attached to it like an umbilical cord is a perpetual queue of dazed clients, and it's the booze they crave rather than the news. And this ain't rhubarb, truffle and caviar-infused premium gin or obsidian barrel-aged rice ale, this is overproof rum which, as the implausibly chipper clerk clarifies, means really strong rum, as in 80% ABV really strong rum. In a cabinet beneath the till is a jar of clear liquid with a faded Dolmio spaghetti sauce sticker around it.

'What's that?' I ask, expecting it to be moonshine.

The clerk eyes me with alarm. 'Just water for cleaning, sir. Not for sale.'

This exploitation of insecurities makes Rough and Ready Clacton a mirror image of the plusher seaside towns we've seen. In Bournemouth there are high-end vets and pet-grooming boutiques that cash in on the moneyed Englander's adulation for animals. The same social group can get a fix of metropolitan sophistication by going to restaurants serving meals on slabs of wood rather than plates, their menus riddled with adjectives like *foraged, curated* and *artisanal*.

Although not plush in the same way, the parts of Clacton west of the pavilion are closer to some ideal of a twee and quirky English seaside town.

2. Twee and Quirky Clacton
The further we progress along Marine Parade West, the more salubrious the housing seems to get. Lately-painted terraces with prim detonations of roses and tulips, some shielded by fences topped with coils of barbed wire. Everywhere George crosses and union flags. On the lawn around a detached mock-Georgian three-bedroomer are thirty well-crafted ceramic statues. A charcoal-toned stag, horse, orangutan and otters face-off with more colourful and conventional garden gnomes with beards and pipes. Behind them a red-coated, tri corner-hatted Napoleonic soldier and a marble-effect Roman goddess in a toga. I can see no unifying theme other than these objects were put here by someone who likes objects that have no unifying theme.

Clacton's unofficial model village

is more coherent. The front garden of a maisonette is crowded with *Star Wars*, Noddy and Snoopy figures, amongst other toys plucked from English childhoods past. Girdling the village is a scale railway with Thomas the Tank Engine half-parked in a green-doored garage. On the maisonette's façade is yet another George cross and a tarpaulin sign thanking the NHS for their Covid response. Next door is that other English icon, the red telephone box, though rendered uncanny by a replica of Michelangelo's David standing inside it. The neighbours are in on the eccentricity, displaying these signs:

> BEWARE OF THE PARROT
> SORRY GONE TO THE PUB –
> TRY AND FIND US
> REMAINS OF TRESPASSERS
> WILL BE PROSECUTED

Maybe such silliness is a legacy of Clacton's salad days when redcoats wowed the post-war crowds at the Butlin's holiday camp. There must be enough Clactonians still alive who fondly recall those tacky times – and others with an ironic liking for them – to justify the nearby Westcliff Theatre putting on a *Best of British TV Comedy* show starring Jeffrey Holland. He's known for *Hi-De-Hi*, an eighties sitcom set in a fifties holiday camp in the barely-fictionalised environs of Crimpton-on-Sea.

Heading back along Marine Parade West, as the North Sea wind picks up

to sting our eyes and chill our sinuses, we find more gentle subversion. A cake tin-shaped Martello tower, built in the early 19th century from bricks and super-strong mortar, has on its roof what looks like a present-day boat cockpit, its sea-facing windows fitted with windscreen wipers. Martellos are relics from another age of anxiety, though the anxiety then was about foreign invasion. At the height of the Napoleonic Wars, seventy-four such towers were built along England's shoreline and kitted out with big guns to repel Frenchmen. An information panel claims that, in recent years, Clacton's tower has been used as a museum, a restaurant and a vantage point by the coastguard and navy. In the 2010s it was, bizarrely, a children's petting zoo.

To get home to our b&b we must negotiate Rough and Ready Clacton again. We're reminded of its rough-and-readiness by a couple of startling sights. The first is a memorial stone to Ian Dibell, an off-duty policeman who was 'killed unlawfully' in 2012. After hearing gunshots near his home, Dibell found the culprit in a car with the windows open. Dibell reached in to try to confiscate the weapon and the man shot him in the scuffle. This is not the only incident showing that the gun crime plague has spread from Greater London out to once-politer spots like Clacton. In separate cases during August 2021, a teenager was detained on firearms possession and drug charges, and a shoplifter was found to be carrying a replica pistol. A fake gun was also used in the armed robbery of a convenience store in 2019.

Our second shock of the day is seeing a woman collapsed on the pavement outside Magic City. She's face-down, the feathery lining of her anorak hood rippling in the wind. Standing over her is a lad in a camouflaged parka like that of a white American domestic terrorist. He is shaking and muttering to himself and therefore not much use to her. Fortunately, a saloon car ambulance arrives and its team check her over. That they don't exactly race her onto the stretcher must mean she's not too serious.

After Twee and Quirky Clacton this is a sobering head-dunk into the ice bucket of reality. Like other seaside towns, Clacton contains multitudes, fuses contrasts, accommodates contradictions. It's hard to get your head round. In the end, are we just a couple of Clactons bumbling cluelessly around a couple of Clactons?

The Hitches of Jaywick
Jaywick, Seawick and St Osyth

As we approach Jaywick along the sparse and sandy, yet wind-battered south Essex coast, I'm weighed down by anxiety. There are several sources of it. I'm worried my reporting will be mistaken for the 'poverty porn' of lurid tabloid splashes and reality TV shows. The headlines swirl around my head: 'The Toughest Seaside Resort in Britain', 'Deprivation-On-Sea', 'Benefits by the Sea'... Then there's the more pressing risk of someone taking a violent dislike to us. Despite our best efforts to keep a low profile, Louis and I have stuck out wherever we've gone in these parts. Well before they hear our voices or see our notebooks and sketch pads, locals instantly twig that we aren't locals. Rubbernecked in every pub in Clacton, we've been forced to devise a system whereby I sit directly in front of Louis so that nosy patrons can't see him draw.

We come to a groyne (a funny term for a narrow jetty-like structure that prevents beach erosion) rolling a few hundred metres into the sea. Halfway up it is the lonely silhouette of a young boy. It's daredevil behaviour – either side of him the water's deep and choppy.

After Jaywick Sands Beach Bar, a bright ginger structure like a storage container, we turn inland onto a main drag of basic one and two-storey homes. The forecourts are littered with guttering, planks, cardboard boxes and busted plastic chairs. We find a Costcutter, a kebab shop, a café with benches outside it and a red tile-roofed pub called Never Say Die. Other amenities have deceptively glamorous names like Eldorado Family Entertainment Centre and Broadway Members Social Club. It's early Sunday morning and we don't see or hear a soul – until a topless guy roars past us on a quad bike.

Further on is Sea Crescent. Not unlike slums Louis and I have visited in Asia and Africa, abodes are spruced up with salvaged – or stolen? – items. A pair of fibreglass pillars are rope-lashed to the front of an ochre-brick house with witch's hat roof. Above is a sign reading 'All Along the Watchtower' and a cartoon of two hirsute guitarists. A string puppet of a red-nosed clown in pantaloons swings from a neighbour's porch. The repurposing is practical as well as aesthetic. In one yard a clapped-out speedboat has been turned into an extra room installed with Calor gas. Snatches of tarpaulin bridge gaps in roofs. Arbitrary tiles and wood scraps have replaced absent gate and wall panels.

George crosses are painted on walls or spasming on flagpoles. A union flag billows next to a star-spangled banner blazoned with WE WILL NEVER

FORGET – a reference to what exactly? 9/11? World Wars I or II? I'd like to ask folks here – but won't – what they think that the UK, America or any other nation-state has ever done for them.

The last rites of a car boot sale are happening in Jaywick Sunspot, a bumpy patch of concrete enclosed by steel music festival-style fencing. One stand has almost nothing legal for sale, from bootleg DVDs to Tesco tennis rackets in their original packaging. We go over to a veg seller, a plum-tomato-cheeked old fellow who's keen to chat. He says investment's coming to the area. There'll be a new covered market. 'It's too posh for Jaywick,' he scoffs. 'No-one round here can afford 200 quid to set up a stall, you know?' He points to a grey-and-white duplex building that couldn't look more out of place next to Sea Crescent's low-altitude housing. 'Been empty since they built it, that. Again, locals can't afford it. Only people who can would be from out of town, and they ain't gonna move here, are they?'

Louis and I go down to the beach, pondering the facilities a community like this might need ahead of craft ale and sourdough focaccia. We've only been in Jaywick an hour and we're sure this is the most deprived place we've ever seen, at least in this country. The stats bear this out – 57% of the denizens rely on benefits. Besides, you know your town might be in a spot of bother when a United Nations poverty investigator decides to visit, which is what happened here in 2018. Professor Philip Alston concluded that Jaywick's woes had nothing to do with personal idleness, and everything to do with years of public underfunding and the Tory government's callous Universal Credit system. Further back in time, when de-industrialisation was killing jobs across Britain's mining and factory belts, the closure of the Butlin's nearby in 1983 condemned subsequent generations to the dole. Indeed, looking around it's hard to fathom how an economy that consists of a few shops, a pub and a greasy spoon could provide enough work for a populace of 5,000.

A bundle of tickets, probably from the funfair at Clacton, blows along the purple shrubs that sparkle across the beach. You need to spend a small fortune on the various arcade machines before you can win enough tickets to trade in for even a meagre prize like a woolly chipmunk. Such dismal odds seem fitting for a place like Jaywick. Louis sits down to draw. I look out to sea and imagine the constituent parts of a poorer, tougher part of the world drifting in and washing up on these shores, in order to make Jaywick resemble the Global South that Louis and I have travelled to, rather than the comfortable Global North that is our home. Perhaps Jaywick is an omen for what the rest of this country will become as Britain's slide continues

amid Brexit aftershocks, a rising China and a floundering America, to whose fortunes we've pegged ourselves for long enough.

At a turnstile between the beach and the Brooklands coastal road, we let two skinny, blunt-faced women pass, prickles of hair dyed crimson and orange respectively. Like weapons being held aloft to ward away enemies, the women grip leashes to terriers that strain impatiently ahead of them. On the road, a father and his ten-year-old both wield Alsatians, the son struggling to control his charge. In fact, the next dozen people we see are with dogs, mostly larger breeds.

We spy signs in windows for Jaywick Sands Happy Club. Founded by Danny Sloggett in 2019, the club is run cooperatively, providing goods and services without money changing hands. If someone needs a place to stay, they come to the club and find someone to put them up. Items can be traded there, from crockery to kids' toys. It's not unlike the truck-driving drifters depicted in the film *Nomadland* who exchange motor parts at roadside get-togethers. At the Happy Club, volunteers organise table tennis and meet-ups for the lonely. Borne out of necessity, the club thrives on a community spirit that has long evaporated from better-off neighbourhoods.

Less symbolic of social cohesion is an amnesty bin into which knives can be dropped without fear of legal comeback. Above the slogan HOLD ON TO A LIFE, NOT A KNIFE! someone has scratched into the enamel coating of the bin in a childish scrawl, NO MORE KNIFE CRIME! The 'o' has been turned into a red 'do not' sign with a diagonal line from upper-left to lower-right. The effect is poignant. Louis and I move on past a one-man tent pitched on a muddy slope with a case of beer in the vestibule.

Half a mile west along the coast, whipped ever harder by the wind and rain, is Martello Beach Holiday Park. Hundreds of chalets speckle the horizon. Some are on stilts with porches and arched front doors, redolent of American prairie homesteads. Others are more like huts from World War II POW camps. We've read that many inside these bare-bones homes aren't tourists – they sign leases for ten or twelve months a year. 'That's one way to deal with the housing crisis,' I quip to Louis.

The sombre, conical Jaywick Martello Tower – after which the holiday park is named – is now an alluring cultural centre. Spurred by the same community ethos as the Happy Club, recent arts projects here have united photographers, painters, musicians, historians and schoolchildren to creatively respond to the theme of flooding and curate an exhibition of beachcombed items from flippers to crabbing nets.

Equally odd objects are on sale at St Osyth's open-air market, just inland from the tower. One stall sells BB guns modelled on real firearms – Remington bolt-action carbines, sniper's rifles with tripods. The camaraderie between the stall-keepers and the punters doesn't extend to Louis and I. If people aren't scowling at us, they're ignoring us.

We speculate as to why. Do they think we're voyeuristic tourists? Government spies come to check they aren't working while claiming benefits? Growing up in a seaside town myself, we hated what we called 'grockles' – rich kids down from London to do watersports for a weekend, only to go home to the metropole and deride our backward ways. Except I doubt if anyone comes to St Osyth to jet-ski, so I'd understand if that adds to the mistrust.

Beyond the protracted rows of chalets is a zone called Seawick. The homes here are even smaller and more dilapidated than Jaywick's. That said, their design and layout prompt Louis and I to wax about relative housing quality. In the UK, where we tend to associate poverty with cramped, high-rise accommodation, we often think that someone can't be too badly-off if they live in a detached house with a front and rear garden. But in the much more spacious US, some of the most blighted ghettoes are suburbs of Los Angeles that look not unlike Jaywick

'Off the grid' is Louis' description.

As with Jaywick, some façades have been flamboyantly burnished. Notes in marker pen on a front window read, LET'S TALK ABOUT ENGLAND, OUR COUNTRY and AMERICA'S POODLE. Before them is a scattering of deckchairs and a half-collapsed umbrella. A banister and a length of green polythene bunting form a makeshift gate. Reminiscent of Clacton's unofficial model village, another garden features some adept sculptures of deer, sheep and Christian saints.

We round a five-a-side football goal that's been left on the pavement and chance upon a car park. An all-purpose store called Dolly's Pantry to the left, the Village Inn Pub to the right. That the latter can't be found on Google Maps stokes our curiosity. It turns out to be a friendly boozer with a long, well-stocked bar overlooked by photos of pop stars from Bob Marley to Tina Turner and Mick Jagger. Louis and I break our rule of not drinking before sundown and order ciders. The publican gives us numbers for local taxi firms – we don't fancy schlepping another four miles back in this vicious weather. When we call the firms, none are prepared to take us to Clacton.

We get directions to another pub called the Tudor Bar, on the end of an arcade covered in day-glo promises that we'll win £500 cash jackpots. The barmaid gives us another taxi number and half an hour later we're edging through the narrow lanes between chalets and caravans; there isn't a direct road to Clacton.

That afternoon, Nigel, the owner of my b&b, shows Louis and I his collection of pictures and documents relating to Essex history. Nigel is fascinated by the 1940s when, as he says, 'there was more of a sense of community. Nowadays people are just out for themselves.'

'Jaywick still seems to have a sense of community,' I reply, before telling him about the Happy Club.

'People in Jaywick have to take more responsibility for their situation,' he says. 'They should learn how to live on a shoestring, like our grandparents did.'

I want to tell him that, in those days, the state massively intervened to help the poorest people, the NHS the paradigm. But what's the point in arguing about it? His view is shared by others in a better position to solve Jaywick's problems, but don't. The local MP, Giles Watling, disagrees with the UN about Universal Credit. For him, it's 'making sure it pays to work and [is] helping people to move into and progress within work.' It's intriguing that Watling, a former actor, starred in the eighties sitcom *Bread*, about the trials of a hard-up Liverpudlian family on benefits. As a devout Brexiteer, he has no qualms about losing

European Regional Development Fund cash worth £1.5 billion a year that has renewed ailing regions just like his own. Nor does he appear to share concerns about flooding with his constituents at the Martello tower, having often voted in parliament against measures to stop climate breakdown.

In our all-too-brief time visiting Jaywick, Seawick and St Osyth, it seems the residents are making the best of a mess not of their own making.

THE SOUTHEAST
Looking Down, Looking Back
Portsmouth, Southsea and Gosport

If you walk around Portsmouth with your head down – take care when you do this, though – you'll see on the ground, in addition to the more obvious roads and pavements, thousands of smaller and fainter paths, trails, grooves, fissures, bumps, ridges, engravings, inscriptions and graffiti. Hailing from different times, these features offer an alternative way of reading the history of Portsmouth. That they intersect, overlap and abut each other in a kind of palimpsest says something about the city's present-day tensions

If you walk around Portsmouth with your head down – take care when you do this, though – you'll see on the ground, in addition to the more obvious roads and pavements, thousands of smaller and fainter paths, trails, grooves, fissures, bumps, ridges, engravings, inscriptions and graffiti. Hailing from different times, these features offer an alternative way of reading the history of Portsmouth. That they intersect, overlap and abut each other in a kind of palimpsest says something about the city's present-day tensions

between nostalgia and progress, insularity and worldliness, conformity and difference.

My neighbourhood straddles these features and the tensions they represent. I live on the frontier between more liberal Southsea and more conservative northern Portsmouth, which from 1979 to 1992 elected Tory Peter Griffiths, infamous for his vividly horrendous catchphrase: 'If you want a n***** for your neighbour vote Labour'. The current MP for the same constituency, Penny Mordaunt, is a Brexit zealot whose scaremongering about Turkey joining the EU was so deceitful that it earned her a tongue-lashing from the leadership of the Conservative Party – quite an accomplishment.

Tramlines (out of order since 1936) weave through the streets near me up to a canal bed dug in the early 1820s. What's left of these passé transport systems are like spectres from the time when Portsmouth was the slipway for global gunboat diplomacy, conquest and colonisation. No other empire has come near the British one's achievements in genocide, racism, social authoritarianism and downright daylight robbery. It was never going to be easy for modern Portsmouthians to deal with their city's collusion in this 'merry dance of death and trade', as Joseph Conrad, who came here as a merchant mariner in the 1880s, dubbed it. Us? We do this kind of thing? Or at least our ancestors did? Well, it depends on what

we mean by 'us' and whose ancestors. We'll come back to that in the next chapter.

Parallel roads called Pretoria and Mafeking venerate battles between the Empire and a correspondingly depraved band of white supremacists, the Boers. The British devised concentration camps especially for this war and dished out the pain on an almost equal and inclusive basis – 20,000 Black Africans and 28,000 white Afrikaners died. 80% of the victims were children. Further north, opposite the railway track is Cumberland Road, a reference to William Augustus, Duke of Cumberland. He earned the sobriquet 'the Butcher' for his scorched earth campaign in the Scottish Highlands in 1746. His troops stabbed and shot already wounded combatants, torched villages full of non-combatants, imprisoned women and hanged over 100 rebel suspects. Two miles further north is Balfour Road, named after he who made the 1917 declaration that began the process of depriving Palestinians of their homeland. The terraced houses on these roads, many of which were erected in the Age of Empire, are today so quiet and placid compared to the atrocities above that they embody the repression of the imperial past in the minds of numerous Portsmouthians – and Britons more widely.

West from here are the cracked paving stones of Winston Churchill Avenue, around which Portsmouth's most powerful institutions are clustered – the council offices, the law courts, the police station, the university. Churchill's graven image has lately taken a pelting from historians who have exposed his 'scientific' racism, support for Greek and Spanish fascism and decisive role in starving three million Bengalis to death. It's worth contrasting the university's decision to rename James Watson hall of residence after they found out the late biologist believed that Black people were genetically inferior to white people... with the failure to rename a street two minutes' walk away honouring someone who put his racist beliefs into devastating practice. Such dissonance speaks to the Churchill Cult's triumph of passion over reason, not to say its mobbish control over the narrative. A local councillor who dared to comment on Winnie's crimes copped violent threats on social media from hard-hat – and no doubt tin-foil-hatted – incels, veterans and that new breed of vigilante who's prepared to hurt a real person if they fear that person wants to hurt a stone depiction of a person who died centuries ago. Hell hath no fury like those forced to consider that they might just be a teeny bit deluded.

Many are drawn to jingoism for its rituals and social happenings. Louis and I observe this first-hand in Old Portsmouth, one of my favourite parts of the city, but not because of the jingoistic

rituals. I love the winter evenings here when the mist hangs above the cobblestones and billows around the mansard roofs and sash windows of houses from the eras of great writers who were born or spent time in Portsmouth: Besant, Dickens, Kipling, Wells and Conan Doyle. The literary atmospherics are completed by the blasts of foghorns from ships in the harbour.

But today isn't like that. It's a bright May afternoon and Louis and I are sitting at a bus stop, watching a platoon of navy veterans who have colonised the pavement outside the Ship Anson pub. Sunburned noses protrude over the rims of pints. The banter is subdued for men of a certain age who are drinking so much. The clue as to why is on their T-shirts. They are gathered here on the fortieth anniversary of the Argentine bombing of HMS *Glasgow* during the Falklands War. Some also wear badges reading LUCKY TO BE ALIVE. There's something particularly tragic about a conflict driven by a sentimental dream of the days when mutton chop sideburns would hurtle 8,000 miles away to defend the boondocks from uppity barbarians. In 1982, Margaret Thatcher came to inspect the fleet in Portsmouth and press-gang the public into this fantasy of making Britain great again as a global player. It bailed out her political career, which till then had been sinking fast.

Where we're sitting now, in an area called The Hard in the southwestern tip of Portsmouth, is a microcosm of the city rammed into a couple of square miles. In that way, it relates to the scaling down of model villages across the seaside. In this tight space is a surplus of stalls flogging seafood, kebabs, fish and chips and other grub people crave after revelling at the old-school boozers hereabouts. The Ship Anson's walls are filled with sepia snaps of warships and its bars decked with red poppies all year round. These taverns have cultivated communities around white, working-class pastimes – karaoke, meat raffles, pub quizzes, pool and darts tournaments.

To our left is Britain's second largest functioning naval base and a historic dockyard containing the restored HMS *Victory* and HMS *Warrior*. Like the Falklands survivors, the *Warrior* signifies some of the absurdities of the imperial project, for almost as soon as the battleship was built in 1861 – at a cost of £50 million in today's money – it was outdated. It saw no action and was decommissioned twenty years later.

In the same period, Portsmouth hosted other boondoggles. Fortifications soon to be ridiculed as 'Palmerston's follies' were erected facing inland rather than the briny deep due to paranoia about the French invading from that direction. Suffice to say, the French never invaded from any direction. The follies, along with the turrets dotting

the southwestern shore, some with original cannon intact, feeds a notion of Portsmouth as a bulwark versus the rest of the world. Did this aggressive topography influence the xenophobia of its MPs?

If The Hard distils the military and reactionary essence of Portsmouth, then Gosport distils it further. To reach this peninsula lolling over the west of Portsmouth Harbour, we must first queue inside a translucent plastic tunnel that's like being inside a giant condom. Excepting that oddity, the ferry station is rather Cold War Chic. (I don't believe this was the designer's intention) It's like a checkpoint on the Iron Curtain where Harry Palmer would make a defector swap. The rusty trumpet-shaped loudspeakers could have been recovered from a Soviet labour camp. A padlocked utility box with a DO NOT USE sign ought to contain cyanide and a silenced pistol.

The ferry itself resembles a torpedo boat, inside and out. The staff wear black and white navyish uniforms. Bolted onto long metal oblongs, the plastic seats are too close together and make passengers look like marines deployed in close formation. To cap the scene off, an old gent twirling a cane and wearing a Panama hat and sunglasses, has red poppy badges pinned all over his blazer breast like medals.

It takes three times as long to wait for the ferry as it does to travel on it. The Gosport terminal sustains the Bomb-era ambiance with a red telephone box and a tacky green and white parallel stripe logo with the seventies-sounding tagline IT'S SHORTER BY WATER. Ads for veteran counselling services and provost training schemes targeting cosmopolitan graduates whisk us back into the militaristic present, in which the armed forces are enjoying a makeover as Avon Ladies for diversity and equality after the decidedly unpretty bloodbaths of Iraq, Afghanistan, Libya and Yemen.

This isn't the only tension Louis and I are aware of as we quit the terminal. Gosport is, as it were, pulling in opposite directions. There's a desire to make it a seaside spot. It has a crazy paving promenade, palm trees, honeysuckle beds and a dainty fountain in a square. The marina, a deciduous forest of yacht masts, adds to the leisurely atmosphere. But like weeds invading a rose garden, these elements are under siege from the prosaic pressures of the local economy. Behind and beside the promenade loom dreary warehouses with iron gates, an angular grey horizon of battleships and high-rises straight from the Eastern bloc, though striped in faded red, white and blue paint.

Like a gameshow host, Louis shows his palms to what he declares 'the image of the day'. It's a bust of former Admiral of the Fleet Sir John Fieldhouse and the peak of his cap is

stained with years' worth of bird shit.
That nobody has thought to clean him
up signifies another tension. Those
who present themselves as friends of
the forces and are eager to bask in their
reflected glory – I'm thinking mostly of
politicians – are at the same time reluc-
tant to protect their interests especially
when it involves spending money on
veterans' welfare, for example.

Looked at from another angle,
the pooh dripping over Sir John's head
could have been spray-painted by an
anarchist or anti-imperial protestor.
The spirit of defiance may seem anath-
ema to Portsmouth, Southsea and
Gosport. But it's there if only hard to
find, like that ghostly web of notches
and niches that overlays the streets.

Looking Up, Looking Forward
Portsmouth and Southsea (continued)

If you ascend any tall building on the Southsea coast – most safely done by lift or staircase, of course – and look north, you'll see a jumbled skyline that charts the same tensions addressed in the last chapter. While the great white pediments and porticos of the Guildhall and Park Building beckon to an imperial reverie, to the east is a newer edifice of yellow mosaic design that smacks of pixelated videogame graphics. Fitting, perhaps, for a student hall of residence. For me, this building dissents from the late Victorian values implied by its neighbours, for the expansion of Portsmouth University since the 1990s has boosted diversity – in terms of both ethnic make-up and political attitudes. (The student vote was crucial to the Portsmouth South constituency electing its first ever Labour MP in 2017, even if said MP has since become a disciple of the Tory-lite Starmer Project).

One showery morning, Louis and I take the lift up 557 feet to the viewing deck of the vulva-shaped Spinnaker Tower and search out an obscure landmark proving that Portsmouth was multi-ethnic long before the university existed. With the aid of binoculars we find a muddy plot of headstones like stained and crooked teeth. It's enclosed by a red brick wall and, sadly, barbed wire. This is the graveyard on what used to be called Jews' Lane, but is now Fawcett Road. I've been there twice to search for my ancestors, but was stymied. I don't know Hebrew and many of the memorials are so old as to be illegible. Some of them date back to 1749.

During the Napoleonic Wars, large numbers of Jewish businesspeople came to Portsmouth to lend money and sell clothes, watches, jewellery and silver trinkets to soldiers and sailors. By the end of the conflict, Portsmouth was home to one of the four biggest British-Jewish populations outside of London. The local Hebrew Benevolent Institution became nationally influential. By 1841, Portsmouth had elected its first Jewish councillor – there were to be three more by the end of the decade. To this day, four Lord Mayors of Portsmouth have been Jews, unprecedented for a British city.

The story of Portsmouth Jews not only adds some rainbow hues to the wider story of the city but shows that people don't have to accept the prejudices of their time. At the peak of Victorian imperialism, local Jews were leading the struggle for their people's rights at home. Come the 1870s, the campaign had overturned the national ban on Jews attending university and

standing for parliament. Until then, such opportunities were only open to Christians. It's another pillar of Portsmouth's – and indeed Britain's – grand delusion of itself that almost everyone I ever mention this to reacts with shock. Anti-Semitism? Racial segregation? They only did that in other countries, didn't they?

From our vantage point, Louis and I take in the locations – from the east to the west of the city – of other Portsmouth rebellions. From now-elegant Portsea came the printer James Williams, who was gaoled in 1819 for distributing a radical pamphlet that mocked the corruption of the Church, the profligacy of the Prince Regent and the stupidity of politicians such as Viscount Castlereagh. From the 18th to the 20th centuries, the dockyard next door was the site of several mutinies and strikes for better wages and safer conditions. (In the 1850s, the dockyard was such a melting pot that rarely would you have heard English being

not to everyone's pleasure. In 1983, the Greenham Common women marched through the city against the deployment of cruise missiles in the UK. Eight years later, peace activists linked arms and blockaded an arms fair on nearby Whale Island. In 2013, students helped cancel a BAE Systems recruitment event at the university. While BAE remain a lucrative local concern, they are now so PR-sensitive as to hide their premises amongst the gun metal-grey business units and security-gated warehouses much further north in nondescript Airport Service Road.

The imperialism that the weapons sector has underwritten for centuries helped implant other diasporas in Portsmouth. In the 18th and 19th centuries, Africans were recruited from the colonies to come and work as sailors and soldiers in Portsmouth. The marketing departments of the military-industrial complex have tried to spin this as military service promoting equality and diversity. But this omits the fact that these servicemen of colour were deployed to go and kill other people of colour around the world for the financial gain of a tiny white elite based in cities, including Portsmouth.

Other nationalities have come here to avoid non-British imperialism. Long before Ukrainian refugees, in 1832 over 200 Polish soldiers fled Russian recriminations after failing to overthrow the then Tsar. Ordinary Portsmouthians not only welcomed them but fund-raised for their food and shelter. As a journalist noted at the time, 'Not the rich and great alone have contributed, but perhaps many a hard-earned shilling has been dropped into the subscription boxes by the artisan or labourer.' The exiles set up what is now thought to have been the first Polish population in Britain.

In Portsmouth today, the largest BME community is Bangladeshi (1.8% of residents), which produced the Bollywood starlet Geeta Basra. Other sizable groups are African, Indian and Chinese. Over 100 languages can be heard around town, with Polish the most commonly spoken non-English tongue. The next most prominent are Bengali (including Sylheti and Chatgaya) and Chinese languages other than Mandarin and Arabic.

These days, the pluralism of one definition of culture is matched by the

pluralism of another. When I left the Portsmouth area in 1998, there was next to no art, music or literary scene. A music promoter I knew at the time damned the city as a 'cultural desert'. But in the last ten or fifteen years, it's acquired a yearly music festival, two more galleries, studio spaces available to makers, half a dozen regular spoken word events, and so much else. We even have our own celebrity street artist, My Dog Sighs.

If all the above is true why has there always been – and remains – a supposition that Portsmouth is a stale, boring, jingoistic, monocultural and, as one of my students put it recently, 'white' town? One answer is that this assumption is often held by those who have never been there. When meeting someone new while living in places like London and Norwich, I'd eventually tell them that I came from near Portsmouth and the reaction would range from a jeer to a frown. I remember one guy exclaiming, 'Jesus Christ, how awful for you,' after telling me he was from... Peterborough. To this day, like some magic incantation, the mere mention of Portsmouth to certain stuffed shirts who have barely left Hampstead Village will elicit a smirk or rotation of the eyes.

One-sided verdicts on the city have also been delivered by those who have at least visited. 'All you got in Portsmouth was the clap,' concluded the comedian Spike Milligan after years of treading its music hall boards. In a hulking generalisation, novelist Henry James wrote, 'Portsmouth is dirty, but it is also dull.' Popping in while on a Britain-wide trip in 1980, travel writer Paul Theroux made the equally sweeping claim that 'History had not altered Portsmouth, much less enhanced it.' In her classic fiction *Mansfield Park*, Jane Austen had one of her characters warn another, 'My dear little creature, do not stay at Portsmouth to lose your pretty looks. Those vile sea-breezes are the ruin of beauty and health.' Not an attitude that's endured, judging from all the women sunbathers on Southsea beach these days. Such negativity dies hard, for more recently Boris Johnson knocked Portsmouth for being 'too full of drugs, obesity, underachievement and Labour MPs.' Not that anyone should care what he thinks.

Such smears came to be internalised. By the late 1970s, the Portsmouth Tourist Board was so short on self-esteem that it published a brochure with the tagline: 'Portsmouth offers thousands of French restaurants... and they're only a few hours' sailing away.' As a rule, though, the more time you spend in Portsmouth the fonder you'll grow of it. Sir Arthur Conan Doyle, who was a resident for eight years, glowed, 'With its imperial associations, Southsea is a glorious place; Portsmouth a town where I know nobody, and no-

body knows me.' The journalist Christopher Hitchens, who grew up here in the 1950s, praised the presence of 'one of the world's most astonishing natural harbours, rivalling even Valletta in the way that it commands the Channel approaches to the Atlantic and the North Sea, and it looms over the French coast while sheltering in the lee of the Isle of Wight, which the conquering Romans once named Vectis.' This opinion might be overly kind – Hitchens was a lifelong alcoholic, after all.

There have been moves to integrate the clashing perspectives I've mentioned, to call a truce between the froth-lipped flag-shagger and the righteous radical. The results so far have been mixed. While Portsmouth Pride celebrations grow bigger and louder every year, if the organisers really were for solidarity and human rights, they wouldn't court sponsorship from BAE Systems who sell their lethal gear to Middle Eastern regimes that persecute their LGBT+ inhabitants. With an exhibition at the dockyard, the Royal Navy has tried to 'wokewash' itself as having helped end Britain's involvement in the Atlantic slave trade. But this partisan history forgets that the navy spent the preceding 200-odd years enabling the kidnap and murder of millions of Africans. It's also quiet on its own complicity in modern imperial and racialised wars against Arab nations.

For me, the awkwardness is best summed up by a work of street art by NZIE sited near where I live. Its giant red-painted '75' refers to the anniversary of the D-Day landings, 1944. While World War II is about the only conflict that right-wingers and most left-wingers can still agree was just and righteous, there are uncomfortable truths that neither side likes to admit. The great showdown with Nazism would have been a lot less bloody if British and American capitalism hadn't spent the 1930s bankrolling and co-building Hitler's military machine. And Britain's contribution to the war in Europe – D-Day included – was minor compared to the Russians', yet present hostilities with Putin means we daren't acknowledge this. I don't know whether NZIE is aware of these bugs in the official fairy tale, but his tribute is weirdly muted. There's no mention of the word 'D-Day' anywhere on the painting. A union flag flutters from the dinghy carrying the troops, but cuts off at the edge of the brick wall so that only a third of it is visible. Finally, the location of the piece is hardly prominent – in a dingy alleyway between Clarkes Road, no doubt named after some colonialist spectre from the Portsmouth past, and the Pompey Centre shopping precinct, its fast food, bargain buys and cash-strapped customers firmly of the Portsmouth present.

I look up and down at this city and I see more work to be done, more honest reflection on what all these images and statues and street names and structures mean – or should mean – to us today.

Guildhall

Coast of Waste
Eastney, Milton, Southsea

In 2007, I went to a beach and had a premonition of dystopia. Carita on the west coast of Java, Indonesia, on that chokingly humid July morning was for me a brief and bitter taste of a future that humanity must avoid. Plastic bags, boxes and wrappers – plus the odd rusty, dented oil drum – rode the sluggish waves onto the black sand. While locals were picnicking amid more rubbish on the beach, they were too wise to swim in the water. My most vivid memory of Carita sums up the irony of human-made waste's attack on nature: untold empty packets of *krupuk*, a starch snack flavoured with long-dead fish, congealed into a plasticky mush that was now harming still-live fish. Fourteen years later almost to the day, I'm standing on the Milton side of Langstone Bay in Portsmouth and relieved it's not as bad as Carita was. But it's not immaculate either. Along the strandline is a cordon of seaweed that has trapped and absorbed garishly fonted chocolate bar wrappers, the polythene lid from a Tesco spicy chicken salad, the ripped-off corners of sweet packets and two languidly deflated party balloons. Louis and I ponder these items' backstories. How did a balloon from a children's birthday end up here? What a journey.

In 2007, I went to a beach and had a premonition of dystopia. Carita on the west coast of Java, Indonesia, on that chokingly humid July morning was for me a brief and bitter taste of a future that humanity must avoid. Plastic bags, boxes and wrappers – plus the odd rusty, dented oil drum – rode the sluggish waves onto the black sand. While locals were picnicking amid more rubbish on the beach, they were too wise to swim in the water. My most vivid memory of Carita sums up the irony of human-made waste's attack on nature: untold empty packets of *krupuk*, a starch snack flavoured with long-dead fish, congealed into a plasticky mush that was now harming still-live fish. Fourteen years later almost to the day, I'm standing on the Milton side of Langstone Bay in Portsmouth and relieved it's not as bad as Carita was. But it's not immaculate either. Along the strandline is a cordon of seaweed that has trapped and absorbed garishly fonted chocolate bar wrappers, the polythene lid from a Tesco spicy chicken salad, the ripped-off corners of sweet packets and two languidly deflated party balloons. Louis and I ponder these items' backstories. How did a balloon from a children's birthday end up here? What a journey.

Two women on a morning stroll say they haven't seen any plastic waste at all, only glass bottles and tin cans. Louis and I puzzle over this before realising that the strandline is a good 20 feet up from the section of the beach people walk along. And even if they did follow the seaweed trail, are passers-by so used to seeing small refuse that they don't register it as out of the ordinary? Or the confusion could be down to some natural objects resembling plastic ones – the white of a cuttlefish skin has an artificial sheen and could be mistaken for a lid, while seashells might be confused with human-built caps and stoppers.

Further along, where the beach elevates into grassy dunes, is a rock pool with a shipwreck vibe. Metal poles like masts and rudder-like rings poke through the water's surface. But these aren't boat components, they're building materials, as is a plastics-packed carpet tile stuck to the pool's bed. This stuff must have been fly-tipped, as most of it's too heavy to have been borne on the waves. On any moral scale of littering, fly-tipping must come low – or at least lower than discarding the takeaway bags and boxes that account for 70% of plastic pollution on British shores.

Opposite the despoiled rock pool, the low-tide marshes are healthy enough to support a sprightly pageant of swans who pester us as Louis sits and draws. Fifty feet out into the water

a latex glove is positioned as if someone is reaching out from under the mud. Nearby is a half-submerged pink frisbee, as if the glove-owner was playing with it before falling foul of the marsh. Then comes the biggest single piece of plastic trash we'll see on our trip – an abandoned fibreglass runabout. According to the women, it's 'been there for years and years.'

The proximity of Eastney Marina could explain the presence of this diminutive ghost ship, along with a rectangle of beige plastic – that looks to have fallen off another vessel – forming an askew bridge over one of the labyrinthine, tidal channels.

Eastney and Southsea Beaches

look cleaner, but the higher tide could be masking the sorts of blemishes on display at Milton. Father-and-son fishermen, their rods arching high into the midday sparkle of the sea, tell us that, of all the beaches they like to hunt off, Southsea's is by far the dirtiest.

'The plastic situation's bad now,' says the fortysomething son. 'If you were to pick through the stones here, you'd find plenty of that crap.' Does plastic ever get caught up with his fishing line? 'Oh yeah.'

'When the holidaymakers are down, it's terrible,' says his eightysomething dad. 'It's all about money.

It's cheaper to have plastic packaging and all that, but there's not a care in the world about what happens after.' What can be done?

'I applaud the litter picking groups you see round here,' says the son. He points to his dad. 'And they didn't have plastic bags in the forties and fifties when he was growing up. Perhaps we can get back to paper ones.'

As we move on, I'm haunted by what the younger fisherman said about hidden waste. Before this trip, I'd read that microplastics – so small as to be invisible to the human eye – can seriously injure wildlife. I wince at seagulls pecking at a bloated tangle of seaweed.

As we near the parts of Southsea Beach where people flock to eat and

drink, we spot, again on the strandline, washed-up plastic straws (banned in the UK since October 2020). There are also polythene shards of various length and width; some like shoelaces, others like flags. At the foot of the concrete slope before the war memorial are coffee cups, more sweet wrappers and a couple of those tiny translucent tubes that cigarette filters come in. More straws mar Clarence Pier, in addition to cream-coloured bottle caps that can't at first glance be told apart from the stones.

While a vast Isle of Wight ferry casts its shadow over us, we look over the guardrail of the Point into the water lapping the wall. Again, sadly, the seaweed has attracted the

worst of the waste. Standing out from the fast-food beaker (with plastic lid intact) entwined by the seaweed and the now-ubiquitous bottle tops is a bigger item whose origin I can't figure out. It's patently plastic, though, and honey-coloured, barrel-shaped and fist-sized.

The dispiriting climax to our journey is the sluice gate in the harbour. From all over the region – and not least Gunwharf Quays mall, the commercial heart of Portsmouth – the sluice has sucked up a veritable bonanza – serrated chunks of polystyrene, a polypropylene takeaway fork, a spray can with plastic nozzle, numerous small boat parts, two mineral water bottles, a condom wrapper. That final object reminds me that plastic waste has come to infect our most intimate bodily functions – it has been found in foetuses.

In Gunwharf itself, I have another premonition of sorts. It's triggered by the knowledge that every single piece of plastic ever created is still on our planet and that if we keep making more it might threaten our very existence. A section of the wharf that's exposed to the water is occupied by remote-control racing boats. In one corner floats a plastic bottle that's absurdly out-of-scale with the boats, which are mini-Wightlink ferries and police launches. Like a 1950s B-movie, I imagine the oversized bottle – to me a symbol of the whole plastic scourge – bobbing over to these vessels – representing human civilisation with its travel, trade, law and so forth – and capsizing them all with a couple of well-timed rams.

A Coast of Fine-Tooth Beachcombing
Langstone Bay

Depressed by all the rubbish I found on the last trip, I want to know what can be done about it. My good friend and colleague at the University of Portsmouth, Dan McCabe is one of a rising number of beachcombers who help to clean the coast. 'If we find plastic we pick it up and put it in the bin,' he says as we trudge the green seaweed-carpeted shingle of Langstone Bay on a steaming June day. 'A lot of people's activities take place on land and others, like sailors and surfers, operate in the sea. You hope they respect their environments. Beachcombers inhabit the space between land and sea and we have to respect it.' On September 15th 2018, Dan was one of hundreds of thousands of people who gathered 20.5 million pounds of waste from the shores of over 100 countries.

Such initiatives, along with volunteer 'beach cleans' across the UK, are pushing back against pollution. Armed with a pincer and rubber gloves, Dan retrieves from the strandline a radiator cap with MADE IN THE NETHERLANDS on it and some clingfilm from a cigarette packet. Further up, the strandline has gone a sickly grey due to a grim variety of waste that beachcombers can't redress. Over the last year, the Southern Water company has dumped thousands of gallons of human faeces, sanitary towels and other delights into the Solent. 'I've watched toilet rolls washing up right here,' Dan says. 'Beachcombers are often the first to see these horrors because we're on the ground when they happen.'

The horrors weren't accidental; they were a business decision. Perversely, it was cheaper for Southern Water to fling the sewage in the sea – and take the hit of a £90-million fine – than to pay for treating it. Amongst the casualties may be the dead crabs we tread past, although the one that looks like it's had a circular chunk bitten out of it has probably been whacked by a predator. A few metres away, a Cancer pagurus has expired with its front claws bound by an alloy of seaweed and shrink wrap.

There is of course more to beachcombing than litter collection. Dan has amassed a trove of oyster shells, hagstones, Victorian bottles (left over from a now obsolete bottle tip), Codd marbles (used to stop fizzy drinks going flat from 1872), 1930s clay mustard pots and barrel-shaped glass Shippam's jars dating from the twenties to the fifties. In its East Walls factory in nearby Chichester, Shippam's manufactured fish pastes – and before that preparations made from Bermudan turtles – that were eaten by generations of Hampshire and Sussex people. As a

graphic designer, Dan loves the typography of the signs and brands on these items.

This afternoon we find intriguing fragments but nothing worth keeping in Dan's view. He doesn't fret if he ends a comb empty-handed. 'It's not a competition,' he says. 'And it's about quality rather than quantity. Whether or not I take anything home, these walks are good for my wellbeing. I connect with nature, clear my head of stress.'

Sometimes beachcombers are humbled by the scale and age of the natural things they discover. Just two months ago, a 6-year-old boy found on Bawdsey Beach, Suffolk a shiny black tooth once belonging to a 20-million-year-old megalodon, or giant shark that would have measured 16-18 metres long. Such blasts from the distant past should remind humans that they were never the first, the biggest or the strongest species on the planet, despite often behaving like they are.

Though Dan would never sell his finds – and certainly not ones like that tooth which should be in museums – plenty of others do. Langstone's antique jars and bottles can go for up to £25 a piece. Literally but in another sense ironically, the beachcombers' El Dorado is a load of plastic. In 2003, rare bits of Lego started appearing on beaches in Devon and Cornwall. The fugitive toys were traced back to the *Tokio Express* cargo ship that, six years before,

had hit cruel weather near Land's End and lost 62 caravan-sized containers to the deep. The Lego pieces were aptly maritime-themed: flippers, life rafts, scuba tanks, spear guns. The rare green dragons and octopuses are today some of the most collectable curios amongst British beachcombers.

Dan's proudest discovery is a lump of charred wood that he uncovered 'mudlarking' – where you scavenge in the mud rather than on the beach – in the Thames near the Globe Theatre. He suspects it goes back to the Great Fire of London, 1666. 'There's a story behind everything you find,' he says. In this way combing inspires his own art, which often focuses on historical events.

Dan also appreciates nature's creativity. He pauses and reaches down to a thing of beauty that my untrained eye has missed. It's a perfectly smooth, silvery triangle of glass. 'Sometimes the ocean fashions something that looks like it's been crafted by a human,' he says. 'This looks so good because it's been washed and bashed and contoured for who knows how long.'

Nature also aids beachcombers by, as Dan puts it, 'sorting objects out by size and weight. The waves will transport the lighter things higher up the beach. The heavier, often more interesting stuff will be nearer the water'. But some round here aren't satisfied with what the ocean gifts them. Dan tells of a local man who has dug holes – some of them 8-feet deep – in the land behind the sea wall. He's unearthed tiles, silver spoons and even World War II medals that he's sold on for tidy profits. There are problems with this. Firstly, the land isn't his, it belongs to a farmer who's tried to bring the law down on our Poundshop Indiana Jones. 'When the rozzers come,' he once told Dan with a cunning wink, 'I just jump on me bike and scarper!' My mental portrait of him morphs into a spiv from an Ealing comedy.

The other problem is that his holes are weakening the sea wall, which has already collapsed at one point, letting the salty water in. It's quite a sight when we come across it. A stream skulks from the sea, courses through the shingle and fans out into the vegetation. All that's left of the wall are snaggy hunks of concrete like huge broken teeth. Black seaweed clings parasitically to fences and the roots of trees.

The farmer can't afford to fix the wall himself, so the Council have stepped in. But the damage has already been done – the field is now a marsh. The farmer's cattle can't graze. He can't make a living.

The farmer's plight is a parable for our times. Beat a nest of snakes and you'll get bitten. Beat the ecosystem and the sea levels will rise. Don't protect yourself and the sea will beat you back inland. In the case of Langstone, the failure to protect is compounded by the greed of that beachcomber. But luckily, most beachcombers harmonise with nature. We need them.

The Porcupines of Fantasy Island
Eastney to Hayling

One reason I wrote a book about seaside towns is that I grew up in one. At the close of World War II, my maternal grandparents set up home on Hayling Island, separated from the eastern tip of Portsmouth by just 500 metres of water. Almost eighty years later, Louis and I are walking through the Eastney district of Portsmouth to the ferry that crosses that stretch of water.

It's the weekend of the Queen's Platinum Jubilee and the flags are out

One reason I wrote a book about seaside towns is that I grew up in one. At the close of World War II, my maternal grandparents set up home on Hayling Island, separated from the eastern tip of Portsmouth by just 500 metres of water. Almost eighty years later, Louis and I are walking through the Eastney district of Portsmouth to the ferry that crosses that stretch of water.

It's the weekend of the Queen's Platinum Jubilee and the flags are out

in force. On Highland Road – a charming assortment of second-hand record shops and bookshops (dying breeds, of course) and independent eateries – we see a union flag with Her Maj's portrait in its centre fluttering from an outdoor café table. Scrawled on the tabletop is BE YOURSELF, BE DIFFERENT. I can't think of an event less likely to promote individualism than a celebration of medieval hierarchy. As a Bennite socialist, my grandmother would be reaching for the sick-bag if she were here today.

As we near the ferry port, the buildings seem not only out of time and place, but unreal, as if they belong to different fantasies of England. The blocks of flats on Fort Cumberland Road fit the utopian impulse behind the creation of housing estates after the war. The dwellings have enviable sea views and are nested in plenty of lawn. Neighbours chat merrily across balconies to one another. For kids there's a large playground in good nick. It's all a far cry from the more popular perception – often not without roots in the truth – of urban housing estates as cramped, decayed, unsociable.

Beyond the playground the mood switches at Fraser Range, a ruined naval facility. I love it because, as we've established, I'm weird and it evokes a sci-fi laboratory that's spawned an apocalyptic virus. Granted, such scenarios feel less like the stuff of fiction these days. Behind forebidding barbed wire

gates with warnings about guard dogs hanging crookedly off them, a lonely, two-storey, flat-roofed structure has few doors and only cracked windows left. Vans with radars on their roofs are parked outside. But Fraser Range's destiny is all-too-prosaic – it'll soon be adapted into homes unaffordable to those who most need them.

Northeast of here, the land contracts into a cape no wider than 300 yards. At its tip is Eastney Landing from where the ferry departs. We join the line of tanned and fit-looking folks who are like contemporary explorers in their sun hats, multi-pocket trousers and camouflage backpacks.

The boat is crewed by large men with stubble and shaven heads – the overall spikiness makes me think of a porcupine. I know nowadays that a shaven head doesn't necessarily augur violence, but I'm old enough to remember when it invariably did. As a teenager in the 1990s, I was often taunted or my friends – never me, luckily – assaulted in pubs or at bus stops by men of this description. They subscribed to a vision of Little England that had come as near as possible to realisation on Hayling Island.

When they moved to Hayling in 1945, my grandparents were looking forward to a more benign aspect of that vision: a serene setting of farms, barns, meadows, dirt tracks, mousey vicars eating scones and bubbly bobbies on

bicycles. This – anything – would have been preferable to Portsmouth during the Blitz, when the Luftwaffe killed 930 civilians and demolished one in ten of the city's houses. Indeed, one night in early 1941 my gran got back to her neighbourhood to find her own house flattened in this manner. She had just finished her shift as a Civil Defence operative tasked with protecting Portsmouth from Nazi bombs.

Hayling's romance soon dissipated when Gran found that most Islanders were firebrand Tories. As a metric of how reactionary the place was then, the only foreign immigrant it welcomed was Princess Yourievskaya, a member of the Russian royal family who'd fled the Bolshevik revolution to settle somewhere even more right-wing than Tsarist Moscow. She died in one of the many old people's homes on the island in 1959.

Hayling must have been even less agreeable for Gran when my grandfather passed prematurely in 1966, leaving her to bring up five children solo. Like a Martello tower standing firm in a storm, Hayling was impervious to the winds of countercultural change blowing in the sixties and seventies. This made my progressive-minded mother, aunts and uncle hate growing up there. Why three out of five of them opted to move back in adulthood and inflict it, not only on themselves again but also on their children, remains an enigma.

I've learned the hard way that, to avoid family arguments, the enigma is better left unpicked.

I have a similar dilemma about whether to challenge one of the porcupines on the ferry once we've set off. He's talking about travel to a friend of mine who's with his bike – there are fewer prettier places to cycle than Hayling, in my view. My friend flicks his thumb at me and says, 'Tom's eaten all kinds of bizarre shit in other countries.' He's right – due either to ignorance or limited choice I've munched on both rat and dog in Asia. I'm not proud of it, by the way.

'They say this is how Covid started, right?' Porcupine remarks. I'm always wary when I hear that phrase 'they say', as it excuses the speaker from supporting their statement with any evidence whatsoever.

'Them Chinese are savages,' he continues, oblivious to our eyebrows launching into space. 'They're so backward they eat dogs, they eat anything. It's their... culture, innit?'

I think he wants to say 'race'.

'They're Mongoloids over there.' Yep, he definitely meant to say 'race'. At this moment, I spot a certificate on the door of the cabin stating that the Hayling Ferry won a Havant Small Business Award in 2017. The document is signed by Alan Mak, the local MP – Tory, it goes without saying – and a British-Chinese man. Racists aren't exactly known

for logic.

'And,' continues Porcupine, 'there's so many of them they're a threat to us now. Us in the West.'

I haven't noticed thousands of Chinese wading onto Hayling Beach. This may have something to do with our strict immigration laws, which this yahoo would heartily endorse, wouldn't he?

'We should drop a nuclear bomb on them and be done with it,' he says before picking up a mooring rope as we approach the Hayling jetty, 4 minutes 59 seconds after we left Portsmouth. If this is a joke, it's in stunningly bad taste. Porcupine's poker face says otherwise. The only way he might conceiv-

ably get away with this is if he turns out to be an undercover decolonial sociologist engaged in some surreptitious experiment to measure the prevalence of biological racism among the general public of the south coast of England. But that's about as probable as Hayling Island declaring itself an independent Maoist republic.

My friend and I smirk to each other when we notice a group of students, whom we assume to be Chinese, waiting to board the ferry for the epic voyage back to Portsmouth. Is it too optimistic to hope that spending 4 minutes 59 seconds with these guys might correct some of Porcupine's berserk assumptions? Undoubtedly.

And I doubt he'd talk to them ahead of a white woman who seems to have entered a contest to be the most Little English person in England by wearing a plastic tiara and glittery gown. I'd like to think that in the final of this contest, which should take place at a street party somewhere, she will face off with a man who is so Little English and so giddily enthusiastic about the monarchy that he refuses to believe any of the allegations against Prince Andrew and has dressed up as *him* for the day. While Louis and I trudge along Ferry Road by the glistening marsh they call The Kench, I consider if Porcupine – who must be 20 years older than me – was infected by the virulent strain of conservatism that broke out on Hayling the year I was born, 1979. Growing up, most adults I knew were fanatical Thatcherites. They had hypocritically clambered up the rope ladder of postwar social mobility – a composite of free healthcare, grammar schooling and university education – only to be now slashing that very ladder to ribbons by voting for Tory cuts and privatisation. Suffice to say, these folks were not hugely tolerant of what my family had become by the midst of the decade – divorced and dependent on benefits because, like 4 million other Britons, my parents couldn't get work.

Seeing the houseboats on the marsh triggers another memory. It's of a Romany Gypsy girl I knew at middle school who I'll call Leanne. She and her family lived on a houseboat, as my mum and dad had before I was born. This wasn't the only thing we had in common. We both wore hand-me-down clothes and were entitled to state-funded lunches – what we called 'free school dinners'. Neither of us could afford to fit in with our schoolmates who wore brand new Reebok Pump trainers, put expensive gel in their hair to emulate footballers like Chris Waddle and went on package holidays to Mallorca. By contrast, our families bought our clothes from jumble sales, our mums cut our hair and in the summer we'd be lucky to spend a day at the funfair.

The crucial difference between us, though, was that Leanne got bullied and I didn't. I think the reason is that, in addition to being poor, she was darker skinned than all the other kids.

One morning, Leanne brought into the school a letter of complaint from her mum. The teacher read the whole thing out to the class, which struck me even then as not the most tactful approach to conflict resolution. As the charges were laid out, I watched the tears gather in Leanne's eyes.

'Paul Grayson called her a skanky gaylord and locked her in the stationery cupboard. Sharon Williams dropped two pence on the floor and shouted at Leanne to pick it up because her family needed it. Six kids held her down and peanutted her for being smelly. Karl and Joe Turner have bushed her three times – they are real baddies. She gets teased by everyone for living on a houseboat.' ('Peanutting' was a potentially fatal move in which the victim's tie would be suddenly tightened around their neck. 'Bushing' was shoving someone into the thorn bush outside the school gates).

As the teacher read on, the other kids stifled laughter. I grew angrier the more I saw Leanne crying and the more I heard the other kids tittering behind their hands. I wish I'd been strong enough to stand up for her in some way. Her fate could so easily have been mine. The marsh ends at a cinderblock wall over which rowdy foliage leans and spills like a penned-in crowd at an oversold concert. The forest is one of several birdwatching Arcadias on the island. Somewhere round here, a country fête took place in about 1990 that was, like the Leanne incident, to re-shape my worldview.

One summer evening, my mum took my younger brother and cousin to aforesaid fête while I stayed at home preferring to write and draw war comics. When they returned to the house, my brother and cousin were uncharacteristically silent. After they went to play upstairs, my mum started crying.

'They wanted to go on the fairground rides,' she sobbed. 'I couldn't afford it. All their friends were but I...'

When I put my arm round my mum's waist, I had the sharp instinct that this was all wrong. My mum loved us as much as any other mum and was doing as good a job raising us. Why, then, were we kids not entitled to the same basic joys – a five-minute jaunt in a toy helicopter or anything else – as our peers?

You didn't have to be a precocious Thatcher's Child to realise that, like a shit-kicking town in Alabama, on Hayling everyone knew everyone else, outsiders weren't welcome and a handful of dubious bigwigs ran everything. Freemasons were alleged to own most of the property. Rumour had it that, motivated by the Masonic creed, they raised the rent on the only shop on Hayling owned by a Black man. Priced out, he closed down and left.

At that time on Hayling, there were other belief systems as deranged as Freemasonry, if not as toxic. Several years before the world was first treated to the wacky notions of David Icke, an eccentric local 'historian' self-published books asserting that:

1. Jesus had travelled all the way from Jerusalem to Hayling Island in 29 AD;

2. The Ark of the Covenant was hidden inside a church that was now underwater due to flooding. Thus, the Ark is today inaccessible to anyone who might bother to verify the theory – how convenient for the oddball who pushed it.

One concession my family made to suburban norms was the occasional visit to Sinah Warren Holiday Camp. Now, as Louis and I acknowledge when we pass by, it's a chicer haunt called Sinah Warren Hotel. It has a spa, 'market kitchen' and 'garden chalets'. But when it was established in the fifties, the camp was the fake jewel in the toy arcade-prize crown of Hayling as a pleasure resort. In those days, wellness meant eating spam fritters every single meal or squatting down to win a knobbly knees competition in which, yes, he or she with the most knobbly knees would win a cash prize. Equality meant that it wasn't just young women who got the chance to be objectified, hence the glamorous grandmother pageants. And childcare consisted of telling your toddler to stop blubbing when they'd fallen head-first into mud off the back of an ass during a donkey derby race. By the 1980s, Sinah and Hayling's three other holiday camps couldn't compete with those package holidays to Mallorca, where an English family could be guaranteed fine weather – as well as the unlimited English beer, full English breakfasts and English fish and chips they could get in any English seaside town.

But my generation wouldn't let go of the idea of Hayling as a beach bum's wonderland, even if the reality was less ritzy. In the summer, lads in parachute-baggy shorts with their hair in ponytails or – this being before the cultural-appropriation taboo – dreadlocks waited for hours in the sand dunes for a wave tall enough to surf on. This seldom happened because this was not Oahu. This was not even Newquay. (Had these wanna-Beach Boys got into a less trendy water sport, they'd have been in the right place. It is an almost interesting fact that Peter Chilvers invented the first windsurfing board on Hayling in 1958).

Despite all the evidence to the contrary, many of my peers thought they were living on Bondi Beach, or near enough, thanks to the extraordinary grip Australian soap operas had over Hayling Islanders in the late eighties/early nineties. Although I was too nerdy for this, my fellow pubescents started bleaching their hair to imitate the almost catatonically laidback surfer dude characters they saw on-screen. They also fell for the cynical mass-branding of stars like Jason Donovan – watch his show, eat the chocolate he endorses, buy his harrowingly awful records. Later in life, a girlfriend to whom I introduced several of my Hayling-based friends remarked that they had their 'own accent', which was 'kind of Australian.' I don't know if this was the result of some aggressive marketing campaign by the Australian tourism board, but in the nineties and noughties almost every Hayling Islander below thirty was heading Down Under,

working in a bar and coming back a few months later with an authentic Aussie twang. This was a strange phenomenon, though not a new one. When a style goes viral, the symptoms can warp our behaviour in intimate ways, including how we talk. During Beatlemania, plummy Home Counties kids would affect Scouse accents. Punk-fixated Americans in the late '70s would drawl and drop their 't's like Johnny Rotten and Joe Strummer.

For me, this escape to Oz says something about the seaside's pull on the imagination. Hayling Islanders at that time were yearning for an idealised version of what they already had but were losing. While coming of age in a declining seaside town they were seduced by a fantasy of a much better one (strictly speaking, *Neighbours'* setting Erinsborough is by a lake). This later inspired them to make the huge effort of travelling 10,000 miles just to find out whether that much better seaside town existed. Concerns about fact versus fiction prompted my middle school headteacher to warn us in one assembly circa 1988 that *Neighbours* and *Home and Away* were 'unrealistic'. He was worried about us making role models of characters who only worked sporadically and precariously in the service sector, and who spent their free time sunbathing, drinking in bars or eating spare ribs straight off a barbecue. Despite all the dissimilarities, Hayling's social set-up was not unlike Summer Bay's. There was – and still is – no industry outside of a few pubs, fewer restaurants and one funfair. Anyone with higher aspirations had to leave – or at least commute to Portsmouth, Southampton or London rather than Brisbane, which was venerated in *Neighbours* as some transcendentally glamorous New Jerusalem. To unwisely mix my religious metaphors, like the Prophet Mohammed, 'Brizzy' was only ever spoken of by characters and never depicted visually. As with Erinsborough, there was zero cultural diversity on Hayling unless you count a Chinese takeaway and an Indian restaurant where it is likely the most popular order was steak and chips – the reflex repast of the terminally unadventurous Little Englander/Little Australian.

For my generation the Aussie idyll crumbled in adolescence. The culture industry was now selling us a rite of passage into young adulthood waypointed by pubs, nightclubs and concert venues. These were in short supply in our sleepy, four-square mile blend of bungalow suburbs, fenced-off farmland and retirement homes, dominated by prissy old-timers who thought that drum and bass had happened sometime in the 1930s between Kansas City and bebop jazz. My peers and I came to despise Hayling and fled to the obvious obverse: hip, bustling university cities.

But that was then and this is now, as the psychoanalysts say. And now, in my early forties, I no longer loathe Hayling, despite everything I've said above and what Louis and I find at the end of our journey. Courtesy of all the porcupines, the street where I grew up, Eastoke Avenue, now has more union flags flapping from it than Shankill Road.

In my teens I wished Hayling would sink into the sea. Now, just as I have started to appreciate certain things about it – the slower pace, the cleaner air, the woods, the beaches, the marshes – it's in danger of actually sinking into the sea given the climate emergency. Is this somehow my fault? Did I strike a Faustian deal that allowed me to escape Hayling and all its delusions at the cost of my hometown's destruction? Even if I were to deny it, I might be obligated to, like a secret service agent is. So you'll never know. Haha.

THE NORTH
Falling Short of Stereotypes
Robin Hood's Bay

I'm a northerner. Sort of. Well, half-northern. Sort of. About 200 years' worth of branches on my dad's family tree have held firm in strong Yorkshire winds. I was named after my great grandfather who was – I am told – a hero in his hometown of Goole, a major port in the East Riding. So much so that – I am also told – if I were to go into a pub in Goole and announce, 'I'm Tommy Sykes' boy', I'd get pints of bitter bought for me all night. I suspect I've been mis-told, though. There's a higher probability that some southern ponce spouting off about his *authentic local ties* would earn himself a well-deserved punch on the nose.

From humble starting blocks, Tommy got ahead in the rat race of the local maritime industry and came to own and skipper his own 250-foot barge. He was a crackerjack navigator. After all, Sykes means 'one who lives near a waterway.' For one birthday after Tommy had retired, his son – my grandad Rowland – gave him a framed copy of the latest *Admiralty Standard Nautical Charts for the Humber Estuary*. Tommy scanned it for thirty seconds and said, 'Rubbish, that.' He pointed out multiple errors, putting the United Kingdom Hydrographic Office's best researchers to shame.

Rowland followed in his old man's wake by becoming a career naval officer. He survived some hefty clashes in the Pacific War and was on one of the cruisers that shelled Normandy before the D-Day landings. Contrary to the modern habit of trumpeting the military past, Rowland never regaled me with boy's own yarns of derring-do. We remain ignorant of what he did on D-Day outside of the terse account I just gave.

That Rowland relocated to Portsmouth, the home of the navy, is at least half the reason why I was born and grew up in a seaside town. If there is a gene for ocean-loving – thalassophilia, to use the formal term – it would be rendered useless by, say, making someone born with that gene walk the plank at an impressionably young age. Similarly, someone born with strong lungs can void that advantage by smoking sixty a day. So it was more a case of nurture, via visits to warships moored in Portsmouth Harbour in the 1960s, amongst other things, that made my dad an excellent hobby sailor and seafaring history buff.

My dad never exposed me to such things, yet I do like the sea because I grew up next to it. But has his side of the family's northern-ness had any impact on me? Not really. I'd hardly travelled further up than Norwich until

embarrassingly late in life. Norfolk, Hampshire and London constituted my England, and I naively concluded that, based on those I'd met in such regions, Englanders – all of them – were curt, sometimes angry and generally unfriendly.

Then I went to Liverpool. I left two days later in a state of what I can only describe as agreeable shock. I'd had myriad strangers wave, wink or smile at me, bid me good morning, wish me good luck or offer me directions to places of interest. One bloke sat down next to me on a bus and told me his life story. It was gob-smackingly tedious, but I appreciated his goodwill anyway. When I later visited Newcastle and Manchester, they were almost as friendly as Liverpool – almost. I had the revelation that English people can be nice to each other, though maybe only the ones up north.

I'd like to think there's a link between such bonhomie and the north's generally more progressive politics. Any city that bans the *Sun* newspaper – as Liverpool has since the late eighties – is alright by me.

I'm eager to learn more about all this as Louis and I drive towards some of Yorkshire's quintessential seaside towns. Counter to the 'it's grim up north' cliché, the North Yorkshire Moors National Park boasts a dramatic spectrum of colours. We may as well have dropped mescaline with Aldous Huxley and opened our cerebral filters to imbibe the transcendent sensory totality of the cosmos. Okay, maybe that's a slight exaggeration.

All the same, we enjoy the bluebell lagoons and the thorny crimson sprinkles and the great pink and purple tapestries of bell heather. The grassland comes in at least five hues of green. The sky is gradated with subtly distinctive blues – turquoise skirting the sun on the horizon, cerulean low in the troposphere, cobalt above and finally indigo at the beguiling apex of our gazes.

Such natural beauty is reproduced at our first destination, Robin Hood's Bay. It's a village of only 1,300 ranged around a lush cliffside. Its core is a Victorian terrace of smart hotels, one of them drenched in not-so-beautiful union flags. At the end of the terrace is a wildly verdant vantage point of the turbulent North Sea. An older, flusher demographic stroll by in numbers. Tanned chaps in white shoes and sweaters tied around their waists may have just come off a golf course. Others are in designer shades, Panama hats and Regatta sailing gear. 'That looks rather good,' says one in Home Countese to Louis as he sketches.

I'm not sure if they're visitors or residents. There's an effort to lure tourists with a banner pitching a 'Victorian Weekend' at Christmastime. 'Why not come in costume?' it requests. 'Games for all the family,' it promises. That

such a gig will not feature child prostitutes and the severely disabled in cages suggests that Robin Hood's Bay, like so many other parts of England, is in thrall to a sanitised edition of the past. Does the very decision to hold a Victorian Weekend imply some value judgement about that era? That life was better back then? Reactionaries would say so. Others, who subconsciously fetishise sex and violence, might be enticed by the model blunderbusses, black frilly dresses and other items sold by Steampunk vendors, who seem to have taken these events hostage in recent years.

The moneyed day-trippers, the flag-waving, the Toryish wistfulness – this is not what I came to the north for. I get enough of that at home, or at least in my hometown on the south coast. Or maybe I'd been expecting the wrong things. Scarborough and Whitby, the constituency to which the Bay belongs, has returned a Conservative MP in 20 out of 22 elections since 1918. 61% of constituents voted Brexit in 2016. This chimes with my great-grandad Tommy, a lifelong working-class Tory who would have been a Leaver had he not been so negligent as to have died twenty years before the referendum.

The nostalgic ambiance chases us through narrow smugglers' streets where union flag bunting has been wrapped round a garden shed. Twee cottages have been converted into pubs and shops with names like 'The Old

Drapery' and 'Bay Fisheries'. I don't – nor want to – know what 'Robin Hood's Bay's Men's Institute' is. It brings to mind the Mel Brooks movie, *Robin Hood: Men in Tights*. But will it be as funny?

We're momentarily pulled back to at least Edwardian times by the toxic yet oddly alluring whiff of a skip full of molten tarmac (invented 1902) ready to be ladled into cracks in the ground. A simulation of the past that starts crumbling is probably not doing its job properly.

We come across a glass-encased noticeboard that could have been nicked from a Laurie Lee novel. At the Women's Institute's next get-together speakers will riff on the topics of 'Who do you think you are?' and 'The luck of the draw.' According to another leaflet, St Stephen's Church will soon be 200 years old and it'll be one hell of a wild, rock 'n' roll celebration when they 'install a large replica sundial above the porch door to replace the one removed in the 1980s.' No doubt Iggy Pop and Oliver Reed had something to do with the disappearance of the original dial. Donations can be made in now almost defunct monetary formats – coins in the church donation box, cheques made out to Bay Museum.

The minutes of the last meeting of Fylingdales Parish Council include a breakdown of 'general expenditure'. £6.65 for the clerk's salary shortfall –

which I hope doesn't represent a day-rate – and £8.16's worth of second-class stamps. This community seems well-to-do so couldn't they stretch to first-class?

We find out more about the mysterious Men's Institute from another notice. It 'looks after an ancient inn gifted to the community to provide a place of quiet recreation to members of the armed forces returning from the battle trenches of World War I.' The use of the present tense here is disarming. I picture 130-year-old veterans staggering wraith-like into the inn for a Woodbine and a Courage Imperial Stout. We read on to discover that nowadays membership of the Men's Institute 'is open to all adult parishioners'. The struggle for women's liberation starts now, sisters – or at least it does in Robin Hood's Bay.

I'm scared that if we go any deeper into the village, we might pass through an energy vortex that will actually send us back through time to 1950. But no, for beyond the noticeboard is some corner of Robin Hood's Bay that will forever be early 2020s. The Higgledy Pig is an upmarket off-licence vending 'England's only carbon-neutral gin', hot artisan pork scratchings and craft beer in abstract-design cans with names like 'Manumission' and 'Neurodiverse Terrapin'. Across the cobbled street a young couple with dad lugging baby on a belly sling exit out of a boutique behind whose windows are locally caught crab sandwiches and 'Yorkshire's first salt-aged and grass-fed beef steaks'.

Louis and I pause on a dry-stone wall bridge to sketch and take notes. A twentysomething who looks like a young Steve Coogan approaches. He's very friendly but despite that, doesn't sound northern. Seeing Louis draw, he tells us he likes to make his own paint out of alcohol and flower petals. He's a good chemist, even if he says so himself, for he now works at a pharmaceutical company that's developing new anti-depressant drugs based on LSD. I hope a passing Women's Institute member doesn't overhear such degenerate libertine talk.

We come away from Robin Hood's Bay disoriented, and not just because of the chit-chat about psychotropic substances. It's a seaside resort with no fairground, pier or other accoutrements. If the littoral siting of Bournemouth allows it to absorb something of the foreign and exotic, Robin Hood's Bay is about as insular as you can get, as per the navel-gazing of the noticeboard messages. Nor are there the economic disparities we've got used to seeing elsewhere on the coast, for Bayers seem not to be short of a few quid. The wealth and patriotism don't square with my idea of the north – or at least how I'd like the north to be. But then why should anyone care what I want, the quasi-semi-hazy-northerner I am?

At Ease With Ourselves
Whitby

Three quarters of the way through our day trip to Whitby, we start to feel relieved. We've settled on an understanding of the place, which eases the job of drawing and writing about it. This is thanks to Whitby having a rounded and coherent identity that, like a conscientious hotel manager faced with indignant, double-booked guests, has been able to accommodate conflicting elements of its long history. The results have wide appeal – Whitby was the UK's most popular tourist destination in 2019.

The revelation hits me after we exit the teeny but compelling Dracula Museum and see posters for ghost walks, spiritual mediums and a festival of Goth music and culture. This supernatural strand to Whitby's character arguably reaches back to the 7th century AD. Then called Streanæshealh, it was the site of the first-ever abbey founded by King Oswy of Northumbria. A little later in 664, the Whitby of Synod brought English Christianity in line with Roman rules governing Easter and the shaving of monks' heads.

But of course, not all mystical belief systems are the same. If these Dark Age holy Joes were here today they'd decry as witchcraft the museum's scale model of the sequence in Bram Stoker's novel *Dracula* when the Count shapeshifts into a dog on Whitby Beach. They'd also object to the demonic voiceover quoting other un-Christian plot points from serial murder to a character calling a crucifix and prayer beads 'objects of deceit'.

While tensions between churchgoers and more esoteric types are rare, 1,000 of the former demanded in 2016 that St Mary's Church shut its cemetery during Whitby Goth Weekend. An online petition bemoaned too many of the eye-linered and the leather-cloaked using the headstones for 'a cheap photo opportunity'. This, it added, was '[disrespectful to] the graves of the ancestors of Whitby residents.'

To the east and above us is a reed-bristling bluff on which stand those very headstones, the tops of which are soot-black. The right half of St Mary's is dilapidated, as if vultures have nibbled around its brickwork. 'You can see how this inspired a classic horror story,' comments Louis. Stoker visited Whitby in 1890 and set three chapters of *Dracula* here. This may only be three out of 27, but you can no more blame Whitby for spuriously capitalising on the literary past than you can Southsea with Dickens (who left town when he was three) or Torquay with Agatha Christie.

I haven't been able to find out if those petitioners successfully banned the Goths from taking their profane selfies. Not exactly on the level of religious tensions you'd find in Jerusalem or Kashmir, this dispute might nonetheless be about the gravest to have lately

from Blackpool to Bournemouth, said, 'England is the native land of the hypocrite.'

Lest the jetty stand accused of being overly white, a Black guy, dreadlocks tucked into a lofty cap, runs a stall selling wire animals he's crafted himself. On the bridge across the harbour, a multi-ethnic group of teens are lining up to tombstone into the water. The girls have no qualms about leaping straight in, whereas the boys take longer to psych themselves up. As always, if it's not caught on camera phone it might as well have not happened.

More dedicated photographers with cameras not built into their phones are busy capturing the swish haunts along Pier Road. The Abbey Wharf Bar and Restaurant has solar panels on its roof. As you'd imagine, locally caught fish and seafood are the big pulls. We enter an eatery called Magpie's that's reputed to serve the best fish and chips in the country. Neither Louis nor I are fans of this seaside staple. We soon realise that this is because we've never tried it in the north of England. Our plaices are soft and succulent – not having been overcooked or frozen for a year – and the light, fresh batter doesn't require a pickaxe to penetrate it. The chips are crispy rather than soggy and the mushy peas taste of... something. The trick is

affected Whitby. Maybe all the visitors' cash helps to harmonise things. As represented by the metal wickerwork statues of old-world fishwives on the harbourside, fishing has been central to the town's economy for about 900 years. It's now been fused neatly with tourism – boats along the jetty by New Quay Road offer wreck, reef, water and shark fishing in the North Sea, not to say longer-range cruises where you might glimpse – rather than kill – seals, porpoises and dolphins. We overhear a captain barking up from his cabin. 'The sun's out, the sea's calm. Come straight down, board and off you go. Do we have any more sailors out there?'

The jetty displays a more disparate range of flags than usual. A union flag with a height-of-Covid-era 'thank you NHS' written into its stripes. A banner with a raver's smiley face against the LGBT+ rainbow. Inevitably, there's the blue and yellow of Ukraine that over this spring has proliferated across English towns, seaside or otherwise. The Italian restaurant we ate at last night claimed in its menu that it was 'standing with Ukraine' whatever that entails. I'd take this virtue signalling more seriously if the same people also flew the flags of the many more countries that Britain's had a hand in destroying. As Bram Stoker's compatriot and contemporary Oscar Wilde, who frequented English seaside towns

frying everything in beef dripping, a waiter informs us. Since that delectable dish, I haven't bothered ordering fish and chips back home in the south.

If Magpie's and its neighbours serve upmarket renditions of regional fare, more affordable northern grub is available. Convenience shops sell shredded beef suet, both canned and frozen. I'm briefly absorbed by a postcard-sized plastic envelope with 'Openshaw's Ploughman's Lunch' printed on it. I puzzle over how you can fit a couple of pickled onions let alone slices of ham, Cheddar and crusty bread into such a modest space. I learn from a cashier that an Openshaw's consists of 'single-use' portions of cheese, crackers and pickle. The same stores have cabinets of handsome homemade pies: pork, steak, chicken and mushroom, mince and onion. Jars of Bovril – the pungent beef stock drink that was once advertised by a sitting pope, Leo XIII – are placed prominently on supermarket shelves. Down south, I've only ever found Bovril and such a plethora of pies served at football matches.

The only risk of drama to our otherwise laidback jaunt comes when we get back to the car park. It's been occupied by bandana'd and Aviator'd bikers revving their Harleys and Triumphs. This too is in keeping with local

Magpies

tradition, as Whitby hatched a major motorcycling group – not gang, I hasten to add – called Whitby 77, now extinct. After its most famous member, Mick Collings aka 'Whitby Mick', died horrifically when a section of the Didcot A Power Station collapsed in February 2016, over 500 bikers massed silently outside Kirkleatham Crematorium in Mick's honour. For folks who are de-fined by the noise they make, this must have been hard work for them, but curiously moving for anyone watching.

I wish they'd give us a minute's silence now. I do find the growl of motorcycle engines intimidating, which I suppose is the point of it. Louis' main concern is the concrete outdoor toilet-dimensioned biker and his per-oxide-blonde partner who've plonked themselves right behind us. But in Whitby's spirit of being at ease with itself, when they see us reversing they give us the thumbs-up and kindly move on.

Make of it What You Will
Scarborough

It's possibly unfair to Scarborough to start its chapter with my scariest memory. But I'm going to do it anyway because, like all writers, I'm desperate to capture your attention and for you not to feel like you've completely wasted your money buying this book. Alternatively, if you borrowed, stole or were given this book, I wouldn't want you to regret that you could have spent your time more rewardingly by reading, for instance, a Jeffrey Archer 'novel' or *Mein Kampf*.

My mention of *Mein Kampf* is not entirely frivolous, for it mildly relates to this memory. It could be partly down to the fact that I am of vaguely Jewish and northern heritage and that Louis tilts with Irish Catholic that neither of us recognised that a flag – a red hand in the centre of a George cross – outside a pub in Scarborough was that of the Ulster province of Ireland.

We learn the pub's political bent the hard way by entering and finding a grotesque array of Loyalist propaganda. We spot the worst first – a T-shirt that reads: FCUK BLOODY SUNDAY – NO APOLOGY – NO SURRENDER. I don't know whether the misspelling of the first word is intentional, but I wouldn't be mortally surprised if it isn't. I'm then distracted by what I initially take

to be an emergency light but realise is a blazing orange – what other colour? – pendant. It honours a march in 1979 by an Orange Order lodge in Manchester. Unavoidably, there are portraits of William himself, who always looks so placid in these pics – it's as if he had no idea about all the strife that would later happen in his name.

I try and make conversation with the barmaid. 'Er, shame about the result the other night.' I'm aware that a few days ago Protestant Glasgow Rangers lost in the Europa League final to Eintracht Frankfurt.

Her eyes plummet below thick false lashes. 'Oh aye, dead unlucky when you lose on penalties.' She sounds more North Yorkshire than Northern Irish. 'We had a full house for that game. We prayed for them but it made owt difference. What can I get you, love?'

'T-two pints of Guinness.' Then I immediately ask myself, is Guinness a wise choice? I think it was founded by a Unionist. Besides, if these hardliners hated 'the black stuff' they wouldn't serve it in the first place, would they? Or is it a ploy to catch out undesirables?

'Anything else, dear?' the barmaid asks. You can't tell much about someone from thirty seconds' interaction with them, but I can't square her charms with the poison dripping from the walls of her pub. But then people

wear different masks for different occasions. Or balaclavas.

I've never drunk a pint of beer quicker. I soon need the facilities. That's a journey I do not wish to repeat. On the walls at the rear of the pub are newspaper clippings that ought to be a source of embarrassment. The headlines shriek:

ALL WELCOME BAR FENIANS
HOME OF THE SEASIDE, FUN FAIRS, DONKEY RIDES, STICKS OF ROCK AND THOUSANDS OF LOYALISTS RANGERS 'FANS' JOIN 8-DAY BENDER AT BIGOTED BAR
POLICE RAID ON LOYALIST PUB

That these are framed and exhibited suggests they make the publican proud. One of the stories discloses that the publican was arrested on suspicion of supporting an illegal paramilitary organisation in advance of a 1,500-strong Orange Order march through Scarborough. A photo shows flinty-faced coppers hauling boxes of documents out of this very pub. However, the article notes, the publican was later released without charge.

This isn't the first seaside town we've been to that's an outpost of prejudice. But if this publican cares so much about keeping Ulster British by any means necessary, why fight for it 300 miles away in a beach town in northeast England with little historical-

ly to do with the Motherland? It makes as much sense as lobbying for Biafran liberation from a tortoise-breeding farm in Uzbekistan.

Perhaps alienation magnetises people towards such crackpot causes, especially if there's some hint that the cause is a lost one, or bespeaks a nobler, more heroic time. Such thoughts have been in my head since we visited the Grand Hotel a couple of hours earlier. Traces of splendour remain in this baroque, V-shaped (in honour of Queen Victoria) edifice which was, when it debuted in 1863, the biggest inn in Europe.

These days it could do with a paint job and some hostile architecture to repel the horde of seagulls nesting in its alcoves and loitering on its window ledges. The screeching, like hundreds of goblins cackling at once, is intolerable – how does any guest sleep at night? While Louis masochistically takes a sound recording of the din, I peek at billboards along the Grand's façade. They point to the problem of what to do with a huge place like this when the salad days are over and you can't bank on the rich and famous to keep you solvent. The Grand's answer is room hire. They can lay on a wedding reception with afternoon tea and sparkling wine for 15 people for £400. Corporate conferences are possible too, with chips and sandwiches provided.

Other modern tastes are catered for when we step inside the spacious

lobby with neo-classical pillars leading up to a wide staircase not unlike the one where Tony Montana made his last stand in *Scarface*. But I don't recall a bingo kiosk being next to the stairs in that movie, so this is one asset the Grand Hotel has over Montana's mansion.

We go into a bar that's redolent of a train station waiting room. Fruit machines wing a glass cabinet full of muffins and digestive biscuits. A not untalented female singer tackles 'Wake Me Up Before You Go-Go' to a synth backing-track of plinking chords and plopping drums. But no one's listening. Ancient as they are, many of the clientele are going into foetal position, sinking ever deeper into leather sofas while stooping forward to finger their phones.

The chanteuse curtsies and that's that for the night. A teen waitress in a black bow tie and waistcoat takes our empties. 'Y'alright there, lads?'
'   Good thanks. Anything else going on in the hotel?'

"Fraid not, love.' She glances sceptically around the patrons. 'Them lot turn in early.'

'Do you like working here? It's a fine-looking building.'

The girl gives an expansive smile that's somewhere on the border between pride and smugness. 'Aye, it's a pretty old place with loads of history and that. Did you know that, yonks and yonks ago, they had taps in the rooms, one what had fresh water and another what had salt water? In them days they thought it were healthy. And the RAF used the hotel for training in the war. It were really important to the effort, like.'

'Can you recommend anywhere to go out in Scarborough?' asks Louis. The girl's expression loses its glow.

'Aww, Scarborough's dead, if you ask me. It's all dead-end jobs and when you've finished for the day, there's nothing to do. I prefer Blackpool, you been there?'

'We'll be going soon.'

'That's champion, that. Went with me boyfriend last week. I got so drunk in this Irish pub called Shenanigans 'cos I'd eaten nowt. So after, we go in a kebab shop and I puke everywhere, I mean everywhere!' She lets out a naughty, deep-pitched laugh.

I appreciate her candour. We've all done silly shit like that at her age, but I recall there being an *omerta* around not revealing that you've puked lest you get a rep as a 'lightweight'. Maybe that's one of the many discontinuities between Gen Y and Gen Z. Who knows and more to the point, who really cares? What I care about – and am grateful for – is people like her who are so eager to chat that they make the journalistic challenge of finding interviewees easier than... finding someone to sing you Wham! songs on a drizzly Tuesday in

Scarborough. Although I know which of those two options I'd prefer.

We quit the Loyalist pub as the barmaid quizzes a scrawny and shoeless octogenarian who apparently doesn't know where he lives, how he got to the pub in the first place or even his own name.

In step with the disenchantment oozing from that pub and from the waitress at the Grand, the following day's roam reveals Scarborough's once-mighty infrastructure struggling to meet current public needs. We find an amusing metaphor for that on the green and hilly approach to the beach. A thirty-foot-high steel ladder, once related to a long-gone railway that in its heyday whisked thousands of holiday-makers a day here, stands lonely and graffiti-spattered on a bluff above the sea, while a hundred yards behind, a male-female couple of metalheads with mullets and sleeveless T-shirts sit on office-style foam armchairs and work their way through a four-pack of lager. In the absence of a pub or café they've decided to make their own social space. As Louis and I watch, we feel uncomfortable, like we're snooping on an intimate moment. We walk on and discuss how far these lovebirds are prepared to blur the line between private and public. After a couple of cans will they start shagging on the armchairs in full view of the passing joggers and BMXers?

Like the ladder, bits of North Bay Promenade wall have outlived their usefulness. We must meticulously time our run past them to avoid the waves lapping over and drenching us. After a clump of pyramid structures that make up Scarborough Sealife Centre, still a big tourist draw, the promenade peters out into a marvellous natural lagoon. Louis and I scale the steep headland that stands between it and the ocean. It's worth the exertion. A couple of miles south on an outcrop are the maudlin vestiges of Scarborough Castle, to its right an undulating chain of pale bay-windowed homes. Directly inshore from us is a mish-mash of council housing and more bay-windowed affairs, some converted to flats, others boarded up.

We head south past some mammoth outdoor venues, empty right now. There's an 11,500-capacity cricket ground and an open-air theatre where Aha, Tears for Fears and other eighties throwbacks are due to play later in the year. Scarborough Bowls Centre is roomier than a country estate, with two crown greens and an indoor rink as big as a football pitch. It's also well-resourced enough to employ a receptionist from 9am to 9pm. I suggest a game to Louis, but he says it looks too boring. The receptionist says we can watch a training session. I try to imagine how one trains for a sport like this. Sub-zero temperature marathon-running?

We're ushered through a veritable complex: restaurant, conference hall, bar-café with pool tables – all in top condition. The only bowling greens I've seen before resemble someone's back garden, albeit finely trimmed – I suspect there aren't enough paying members to fund a joint of this magnitude down south.

Six players stand either side of the indoor rink. The white hair, white shorts and white socks make them almost translucent. Balls are thrown, balls roll. The proceedings are so calm and slow I start to feel stoned. Time brakes.

On the way out, we find an advert for Bowls and Buggies, a bowling club that compassionately caters for the disabled.

'What time is it?' asks Louis.

'2:30.'

'Naah, it should be four at least.'

Nearby, in fragrant Peasholm Park, palm and bonsai trees make for a reverse-colonial atmosphere. Willows weep into a daisy-fringed lagoon leading to an island backgrounded by an East Asian-style pagoda with pedestal and finial crown. A bandstand is done out in the same style but situated in the lagoon itself. It's defunct, a park attendant tells me. I try to picture its glory days when bassoons and cellos would presumably have to be transported there on a pedalo. The pedalos have survived to the present.

Again, it's disappointing to find

such a pretty place underattended on a sunny May afternoon. When we hear a noise that's like sleet against a tin roof, our instinct is to find shelter. Then we clock that the sound is in fact coming from a troop of hi-vis-vested preschoolers chucking coins down a wishing well. Their teacher then tells them to look up at the majestic Scots pine tree. Like an arboreal Catherine wheel, its spoke-like branches culminate in outbursts of needles. After that, the nippers throw bits of stale bread at already rotund geese.

I reflect on whether these kids will grow up short of options, like the waitress or the yahoos in the Loyalist dive – or make some options of their own. Fitting the latter category is the couple who founded Steampuss Cat Lounge down an alley off Scarborough town centre. As the name indicates, this is a lounge full of felines, from small, rodential breeds to the hirsute monstrosities that get themselves fondled by Bond villains. The conceit is that you watch or play with them over a hot or cold drink. A few years ago, Chloe Cotton was a burnt-out primary schoolteacher and her partner Matthew Davenport was sick of working in a call centre. They held their breath and took the plunge into starting a business that's survived lockdowns and cost of living hikes. That's an outcome as cute as the critters they look after – assuming you're a cat person, which Louis and I are.

On our last night in Scarborough, we find another pub that, though directly across the road from the Unionist hangout, is its polar opposite. It is southern Irish-themed, judging from its collages of Eireann pub signs and old cartoons lampooning Dublin politics. An open mic night is in full flow with a rabble-rousing poet in John Cooper Clarke's mould shouting for solidarity amongst the youth and scolding those youths who smoke too much weed and play too many computer games. The punters here look cheerful and bohemian enough not to draw the heat of an anti-terrorism unit. They've found each other and made the best of their environment, which is what we all do wherever we live, I suppose. Would that waitress at the Grand change her mind about Scarborough being 'dead' if she came here? I'd like to think so. I feel like crossing the street and telling the Loyalists to come here and sing a song or recite a poem. It might chill them out. Equally, I might just get a smack in the mouth.

At any rate, Louis and I agree that this is a pleasing way to round off our time in Scarborough.

Steampuss
Cat lounge

Rock-Ups
Bridlington

Folk wisdom says that every person has their doppelgänger somewhere in the world. Does every seaside town have one too? While Bridlington is not identical to Hayling Island, where I was brought up, there are eerie parallels. I start to revise my earlier opinions on the chasm between north and south. But somehow, I feel estranged rather than reassured by experiencing so much that is familiar to me.

Like Hayling, the stretch of Bridlington we visit has a smidge of washed-out Regency houses near the shore, but behind it many more bungalows built later when pop stars dressed as Regency dandies. Both locations have a modest fairground with a shaky-looking big wheel. The way the sea slithers out from Bridlington Beach in longsword shapes during low tide is very Haylingesque. The average age of Hayling Islanders is 40, Bridlingtonians 43. Both have substantial elderly populations – although you could say that about many seaside towns. I'm not aware of the two settlements being twinned or having any other connections.

As with the Motherland, numerous gift shops sell little else but that sticky, crunchy formulation of granulated sugar and glucose syrup that we call rock. Although the first mention of rock

in print dates back to 1652, it took off in the seaside in the late 19th century when canny confectioners started to add lettering to each stick spelling out 'Blackpool' and other such place names.

150 years later, we are in less innocent times as I browse through large, penis-shaped lengths of rock reading SUCK ON THIS and HORNY DEVIL. I ask the shopkeeper, a stocky, bun-haired woman from Middlesbrough, if she worries about kids finding these wares amid the boiled sweets made into more wholesome mock-ups – or rock-ups – of cream cakes, éclairs and doughnuts.

'Blame the boss,' she shrugs.

'Where are the penises made?' I ask.

'Most of them in the Fylde, up in Lancashire.' She raises her eyebrows naughtily. 'All the big ones come from China.'

Of all the indices used to gauge China's ascent to global economic supremacy, this is not one I had imagined.

'What do you recommend?' I ask.

'Coming from further northeast, I like a black bullet,' she says.

Expecting that to be a euphemism, I risk asking what it is anyway.

She holds up a jar of dusky boiled sweets like miniature lumps of coal.

'Anything else you can recommend?'

'Fudge,' she says. 'But I don't like anything too claggy. You know what

claggy is? You probably don't if you're a southerner.'

'Okay then,' I say, 'give me some fudge that's not too claggy.'

The next gift shop puts that one – and any on Hayling – to shame. It must have the largest stash of rock in the known universe. Being a disturbed and unstructured individual, I'm drawn to the rock-ups of meals. Again, there's something uncanny about candy that's been shaped and coloured to resemble the bacon, eggs, sausages and beans of a full English breakfast. I recall this particular rock-up from my Hayling days, but Bridlington has others I've never seen before – a fruit bowl of grapes, bananas, apples and pears, and fish and chips, which looks absolutely nothing like real fish and chips. The fish is closer to a dog's tongue, the chips cigarette ends and the peas bogies. These comical flaws in the simulation are one reason for my fascination. Another is how rock-ups are wrapped with see-through film to a card or plastic plate, as if they're intended to be kept and even hung on walls as souvenirs rather than eaten. (Chewing on one is likely to crack your teeth anyway). Rock-ups certainly far outlast the foodstuffs they depict. My research shows that rock can last for up to a year if stored in a cool place. I suspect longer.

My lengthy inspection of the rock-ups is starting to bore Louis and alarm the cashier. She peers with fear over to the door, perhaps hoping my carer will intervene. 'If you're that interested, love,' she says, 'you should visit John Bull's Rock Factory in Carnaby.'

'What other meals do they do rock versions of?' I ask. I'm almost certainly coming over too enthusiastic now.

'Don't quote me on this but I think they do roast beef and Yorkshire pudding.'

'Roast beef and Yorkshire pudding!' I exclaim. 'Do you have any in stock?'

''Fraid not, love.'

Louis intercedes. 'No dude, we do not have time for a goddamn rock factory.'

When we've left Bridlington, Louis says he needs to restock on pens and sketchpads. We track down a large out-of-town stationer's in an industrial park. While we wait for Louis' order to be collected from the warehouse, an old boy called Sam chats with us. 'Where you lads from then?'

Simultaneously, I say 'Portsmouth' and Louis says 'New York'.

'Oh aye,' says Sam. 'I grew up down there. Not New York but Hayling Island.'

'No way,' I gasp. So 300 miles away from Hayling not only do I stumble upon somewhere that smacks of Hayling, but I meet someone from Hayling.

'Moved down with me parents from Yorkshire when I were a toddler, then came back here at twelve. I were mad on aeroplanes when I lived on Hayling, though. I remember in 1963, when I were ten, going to Havant Station to buy a train ticket to see an air show. When the inspector asked me where I were going, I said, "*Bazz*ingstoke." He laughed and said, "It's pronounced *Bas*ingstoke. You're from the north, aren't you?" I said, "Aye, do you know me dad?"'

I ask him if there are any historical links between Bridlington and Hayling.

'Can't help you there. Not been to either for donkey's.'

As we drive out of the stationer's, I clutch my sickly-sweet fake fish and chips to my chest and wonder how possible it is that Bridlington is a rock-up of Hayling – or vice versa.

Do What We Like and Nobody Minds
Blackpool

'Dr Harold Shipman looked up me arse.'

This is the last thing Louis and I expect to hear from a total stranger in a classic rock-themed bar in Blackpool. He has the archetypal boomer's grey-hair-receding-into-a-ponytail, bald zones danced upon by the neon sign above blinking STAIRWAY TO HEAVEN – SEATING UPSTAIRS. Boomer raises his voice to compete with the droopy-fringed lad on-stage playing a jazzy, stop-start version of 'I Shot the Sheriff' on acoustic guitar.

'Mind if I sit here, lads?' If we were in the south I'd have been suspicious, but this is the amiable north.

'I were working in the Benson and Hedges factory in Manchester,' continues Boomer, sliding onto a stool. 'There were so many of us employees, we had heaps of nurses and GPs who'd see us regular like. And one of the doctors were this Shipman.' Boomer pauses to suck at the head of his Guinness. 'And he were a really nice bloke. Don't get me wrong, he weren't a nice bloke. But he were a nice bloke to me. At *that* time.'

'So why did he look up your arse?' I query. I'm drunk enough now to dispense with niceties. Anyway, I've

learned that Blackpudlians like directness.

'Had this pain down there. So he had a peek and found polyps. Nowt serious, he said. He gimme some meds, it were sorted in a week.'

In keeping with the hair, Boomer's a muso himself. He loves Simon and

Garfunkel, he says. He shows us an iPhone video of him performing 'The Boxer' in a tawdry club in Magaluf, where he went on his son-in-law's stag do last month. I can't imagine this existentialist lament about shame and failure going down well in the decadent party capital of Mallorca. But that's the

quirkiness of seaside towns for you – and not just ones in England.

Louis remarks to Boomer – who still hasn't told us his name and never will – on the masses of live music and theatre venues we've seen in just one evening.

Sooty Show after seeing a urine-yellow bear puppet for sale.

While you can still see VIPs from Steve Coogan, who played the night we met Boomer, to Lady Gaga, who rocked the Blackpool Opera House a few years ago, Louis and I are after something more vernacular. We find it next morning at the Blackpool Tower Ballroom, where cockled couples foxtrot to a Wurlitzer organ that, with its chunky, overhanging keyboard, looks like a deluxe barbecue set. It's being played by a man in a navy blue blazer on a velvet-cushioned stool. He gives me a huge xylophone grin when I approach. As he bashes out 'When the Saints Go Marching In' and 'Bring Me Sunshine', I'm struck by the lavish wall of sound that can be built on a Wurlitzer, even if its whines and wheezes soon start to grate. I glance up and see a motto above the red-carpeted stage: 'Give me discourse, I will enchant thine ear.' I look further up and clock the names of Liszt, Elgar, Chopin and other great composers painted above the Ballroom's opulent golden balconies. What would they have made of this clangour? Schoenberg or Varèse might have just about dug it.

Some of the dancers are good, others really aren't. The much older contingent misstep or spin in the wrong direction or clap at the wrong time or gaze gormlessly up at the ceiling. A gay couple are mismatched, at least in

'All that's from when this town were the heart of world showbiz,' says Boomer proudly.

He's not wrong. At Blackpool's late Victorian zenith, the dazzling ballrooms and concert halls comprising the Winter Gardens and the Blackpool Tower (all still extant) vied to book the biggest – often in more than one sense – opera singers of the time. The Spanish diva Adelina Patti and the Briton Madame Melba commanded fees of £500-600 (about £40-50,000 today). And that was just for a night's work. Think of any great British comedian of the 20th century and chances are they apprenticed in Blackpool. Many are honoured by the singularly zany Comedy Carpet out on the promenade. A feat of typographical design, it's a collage of catchphrases ('Suits you sir!', 'I don't believe it!, 'Ooh matron!) and the names of funny men, women and however else folks may wish to identify. An eight-foot-tall bronze statue of Morecambe and Wise greets you at the stunning Art Deco entrance of the Winter Gardens. The first member of that duo took his stage name from his birthplace Morecambe, another resort up the road. On the northernmost of Blackpool's three piers, a blue plaque marks the spot where, in 1948, Harry Corbett was inspired to devise *The*

absence of anything better. This is often the angle taken by metro media types who condescend to hazard this far up from the Watford Gap. But that isn't our view. We get a strong sense of a community caring about its vulnerable members, with the elderly, lonely and possibly dementia-troubled clearly stimulated by the music and the moving about. There's a kind of punk ethic too, with everyone busting a groove no matter how good or bad they are at it. Around the bar area of the Ballroom are plugs for coffee mornings, book groups, country walks and other public-spirited activities.

Along with 'culture' and 'cre-

ativity', 'community' forms part of the tagline of another venue, the Old Electric, a 20-minute walk south from the Ballroom. From the street it looks like a nightclub with its gleaming black façade and minimalist lettering. Our suspicions seem to be confirmed when we go inside and encounter a blonde woman dressed in the sparkly jacket of a seventies comedian.

'Do you have anything on tonight?' I ask, expecting bingo or off-colour stand-up.

'Not tonight, but our re-imagining of *A Midsummer Night's Dream* is on at the weekend.' She introduces herself as Melanie and tells us that the Old Elec-

tric is an independent, not-for-profit arts centre that puts on music, painting and writing workshops for refugees, recovering addicts and young creatives. It's just one of several new grassroots projects helping to contest Blackpool's boilerplates.

Unlike the bars and clubs around it, the Old Electric doesn't court tourists or party animals. '85% of people who come to us are from Blackpool,' says Melanie. 'We're also not licenced because round here you can get a drink in every single place, including a chemist. That doesn't sit easily with some of the work we do.' Quite – not the most prudent plan to invite alcoholics to a well-stocked bar.

The social trials Melanie alluded to are evident when Louis and I get back on the streets. It's not even 1pm and there are posses of the scalp-mown and brow-tattooed, clasping dented cans of lager and crooked roll-ups. I don't think I've seen so many younger people on mobility scooters or in wheelchairs. There are even more on crutches and walking sticks. Sometimes they too are drinking and smoking. (I make no value judgement here, for I too continue to imbibe despite my health conditions. Millions do, although some have better support when it all goes wrong).

We duck into a minuscule pub

on Talbot Road and find a young man bending almost 45 degrees to inspect the beers on tap. His elbows are blood-smudged and crisscrossed with blade wounds.

The snowman-figured publican shuffles round the bar to confront him.

'I'll not serve you, son.'

The lad cranes his neck up. 'What reason?'

'Had enough.'

The lad pulls coppers out of his tracksuit bottoms, which are sagging.

'Not about money.'

'But I want it.'

'Bugger off now.'

The lad sighs and saunters. When he reaches the door, his trousers are at the thighs.

At no point do Louis and I feel any hostility towards us from any of these people. Quite the opposite. A bit later, a twentyish girl finds us squinting at a bus timetable and briefs us on what's worth seeing. These include attractions worthy of any capital city on Earth – Madame Tussaud's, Ripley's Believe it Or Not, the world's tallest rollercoaster. What isn't worth seeing is Fleetwood, she adds. It's boring, about 7 miles north of here and has nothing to do with that other rocker with grey-hair-receding-into-a-ponytail, Mr Mick Fleetwood.

Like our mate Boomer, Blackpool's amenities are frank and to the point. WE SELL FAGS exclaims a swing sign

on the pavement by a cornershop. WE'VE GOT IT, says another. A greasy spoon café has no name, just a menu: 2 BACON, 2 SAUSAGES, 2 EGGS etc. As you'd expect, Greasy Joe's sells hot dogs, burgers, cheesy chips and that northern *pièce de résistance*, chips and gravy (called, more ritzily, 'disco fries' in New York, Louis informs me). A sweet shop called, plainly, 'Sugar Factory' subverts the venerable marketing dictum that you must be completely dishonest about what you're trying to sell. Eat and Run Café and Takeaway risks being the opposite of marketing if customers take the name as a directive.

At 1.30pm, the Lifeboat Inn is standing room only, in full karaoke swing. The patrons are mostly female retirees, smirks on their gobs, gins and bitter lemons in their paws. In the Irish bar, that our waitress in Scarborough recommended, called – what else? – Shenanigans, the sweat-drenched and gurning are stumble-dancing between beer barrels to Joan Jett, The Specials, Aha. The DJ gives a birthday shout-out and urges us to join 'Play Your Cards Right' this evening, which will be merged with a 'karaoke disco'. Sounds confusing to me. 'First prize is a bottle of bubbly,' says the DJ. The cheer is fully to be expected.

To emerge from all this into broad daylight is even more confusing. 2pm in Blackpool is like 2am in other towns. And it's only a Tuesday.

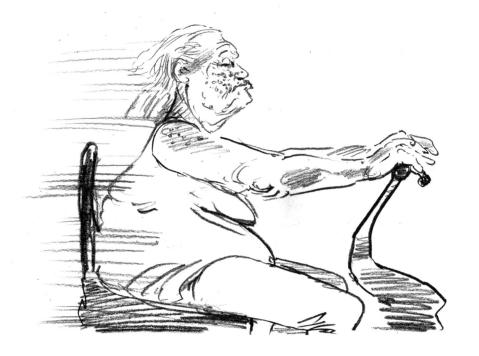

I'm charmed by the shamelessness of it all. It's less hypocritical than posher places where much the same debauchery goes on only behind closed doors and amongst the middle classes, who think that sinking three bottles of 19 Crimes red wine and kvetching about school fees is that much classier.

The next venue we go in seems to epitomise the gap between Blackpool's surface and its substance. From the outside, the Sun Inn looks diabolical, like it's been hit by an air strike – rocket-sized gashes in the wall, bricks on the brink of falling on our heads, fractured windows. But inside it's a trim working-class boozer with an overly affable barmaid.

'What do you want, darling?'
'Two lemonades please.'
'£4.40 please, dear.'
'There you are.'
'Thanks, pet.'
'Thanks.'
'Bye then, sweet.'

We're back almost at the seafront, near Blackpool Tower. It has an industrial feel, more power pylon than the Eiffel Tower that allegedly inspired it. The salmon brickwork at its base is pure Victorian cotton mill. When the proletariat flocked to Blackpool after the Tower went up in 1894, did they so miss the bleak factory towns they'd escaped from that they needed a lanky reminder? Time has made this question redundant, as almost nobody these days works in heavy manufacturing. Sadly, few in these parts would appear to have a job of any kind to go back to – or if they do, they have very tolerant bosses who let them get pissed all day.

Another sight visually similar to the Tower is the six narrow silver structures looming out of a grassy mound on the promenade. With no explanatory plaque about, Louis and I debate what the hell they might be. Giant tusks or teeth defending Blackpool from amphibious menace? There's certainly something bestial about them. Like the fossilised ribs of a dinosaur discovered at an archaeological dig, they could be remnants from the Age of Machines – chimneys or waste pipes or coupling rods.

Those who run seaside towns tend to invest in the parts that tourists spend money in, to the neglect of everywhere else. This can cause a rift between the spruceness of the seafront and the grubbiness you find on pretty much the first street inland. While it's not as severe as walls thrown up to hide slums in the run-up to Olympic Games in the Global South, the same mentality pertains: out of sight, out of mind – for want of a more original phrase. A textbook case of this is where I live in Southsea. Riding my bike around my neighbourhood that's a mile from the sea, I risk a flat tyre from the glut of broken Corona bottles and used nitrous oxide canisters. But down on the coast, the Council deigns to tidy and maintain

the delightful Rose Gardens, Castle Field and Canoe Lake areas... because the higher Council Tax-payers live round there?

Blackpool isn't quite like this. The inequality seems more horizontal than vertical. The further south along the promenade you go, the less elegant things get. It's only a couple of minutes' walk from the Spyglass, a trendy warehouse bar clad with Manhattanesque rectangles of black glass, to hotels costing £15 a night and for good reason. As usual, they have deceptively flashy names: Kensington, New Brooklyn, Sunny Days, Paradise in Blackpool. One has 'brothel' written all over it, if not literally: mirrorball over the doorway, glittering curtains, turquoise and purple spray paint-job and promises of 'bedz and bar'. Another establishment seems to have had most of its fixtures and furnishings stripped and dumped in a skip in its forecourt. Loitering beside it, a man lets his Alsatian discharge an ovaloid turd on the pavement while he vanishes into a cloud of his own vape smoke.

Where there isn't a janky guesthouse or fish and chip shop, there's a living room-sized bingo spot. We drop into Pat's Bingo where it costs 10p a game. We sit in a booth amid prizes that include cuddly toys dangling by their necks from the ceiling as if they've been sentenced to hanging. Pat wears a bucket hat and steamed-up glasses. He

stands in the corner with a microphone muttering the numbers in that rhyming code that tells you a fair bit about the attitudes and interests of bingo-indulgers.

'Old age pension – 65.'
'Heinz varieties – 57.'
'Fat lady with a duck – 82.'
'Fat lady with a crutch – 87.'
'Two fat ladies – 88.'

Before Louis and I have even sussed out how to slide the shutters over each of the numbers in our booth when they're announced, someone calls 'bingo!' and the game is over. This is way too hard for us.

'Aww, but I won ages ago,' complains another of the players.

'Shoulda shouted louder, love,' says Pat. 'Better luck next time.'

Since it's only 10p Louis and I have a last go.

'All red, all there,' says Pat. 'Line 'em up, pop 'em in now.' We haven't a clue what that means. 'Nice low shout when you think you got a win.' Okay, that makes more sense.

Somehow, I win the next round. If you look up 'beginner's luck' in a dictionary of idioms, you ought to see a description of that game beside it. I take my ticket to the desk and discover that I'd need five more just to claim a fridge magnet. To get a lynched toy giraffe I'd need fifty. With one game lasting about 10 minutes, I'd have to spend another 500 hours or almost 21

days playing – and be sure of winning every single damn time. And then I'd likely have to check into Bingo Players' Anonymous.

Having reached peak-promenade with that experience, we dip inland and gawk around Banks Street and Dickson Road. The second-hand shops cater more to the austerity-afflicted than the treasure-seeking, as implied by this handwritten note in a window: 'If you're going to attempt to burgle us, remember to smile as you're on CCTV 24-7. It's recorded to hard drive and viewed from multiple devices very nearby. And yes, the alarm is active.'

The surveillance extends to the town centre where some truly dystopian CCTV cameras echo reptilian aliens with jittery bug-eyes. Ten-foot-high tubular bodies bulge and curve at the top into serpentine heads, on the faces of which are glass bulbs housing home video-style cameras, each swivel this way and that violating yet another civil liberty we probably aren't even aware we're entitled to.

It's funny how a mild shock like this can make you revise your opinion of a place. This sinister tech makes me recall something I'd forgotten about our trip to the North Pier yesterday: the notice that 'prohibits the filming of this attraction' or the capturing of it by 'stills photography' without 'written permission of the management'. That seems not only mean-spirited but

self-defeating, as you'd think business round here would welcome any publicity post-Covid.

Still, I doubt Blackpool is any more authoritarian than any other seaside town we've been to. At least there aren't entire districts sealed off from the public, like the naval base that stares Southsea out from the west. Indeed, Blackpool may be freer in some respects, thanks in part to a veritable LGBT+ quarter around Lord Street and – predictably enough – Queen Street.

After a passable curry – if you want to eat well in Blackpool it's got to be fish and chips or modifications on that motif – we drop into an over-lit cocktail bar called Garlands. A bouffanted drag queen works the DJ booth and a rather

straight-looking young male delivers camp standards from Village People and Earth, Wind and Fire. Reasoning that he won't arouse too many eyebrows at such an alternative hangout as this, Louis produces his sketchbook. We soon attract another stranger. Again, a straight- and square-looking bloke wearing cropped hair and a durable sweater. He stares at Louis with fascination, then sits next to me, says he's Robert.

'Me dad was a painter, like,' he shouts into my ear over the music.

'Do *you* paint?' I ask.

'Oh no...' Robert trails off and looks over to the dancefloor where another drag queen is attempting to breakdance in an enormous sparkly ballroom gown. 'Alright though here, innit?'

'You a regular?'

'Oh no. Just dropped in after me shift. I'm a taxi driver.' He looks back to the attempted breakdancing. 'Good nowadays though, innit?'

'How do you mean?'

Robert nods toward the drag queen, who's now been joined by a couple of bald old-timers in tracksuits. 'It's like, she can come here. I can come here. You can come here. We can go where we like, do what we like and nobody minds.'

I agree. Blackpool's historic showbiz status must have opened it up to different folks with different preferences, so maybe by now tolerance is in the town's DNA. Despite their problems, the people we've met rub along alright, lubricated by the common language of hedonism.

And there are tonnes of fun to be had, with older forms of it tastefully preserved. The world's first electric tram service was built here in 1885 and its route along the promenade remains both viable and iconic thanks to the Council modernising old trams and introducing brand new ones. Similar work has been done on the Illuminations, although the caricatures of bare-arsed showgirls affixed to the lampposts need to be updated by a further four decades. Unlike in so many other resorts, savvy

spending has saved several spectacular spots from superannuation – the curvy, retro-sci-fi proscenium arch of the Blackpool Opera House (1939) is perhaps the most beautiful human-made thing I've seen on all our trips to the seaside.

Whatever the meaning of seaside towns to English culture these days, Blackpool has hung on to its reputation as the greatest seaside town of them all.

Dedication

Tom: To my sisters Lucy and Ella, and brothers Jann and Caspar.

Louis: To my parents who have always been supportive of my artistic endeavours. Even when they didn't understand them.

I'd also like to dedicate this effort to Mario Minichiello who pushed me to find a voice in drawing and a love of observing the world.

Acknowledgements

Hanging out in seaside towns over two summers may seem like not very hard work. But it was quite hard work – honest – and to produce a book out of the experience required a lot of assistance from various individuals and organisations.

Our deepest thanks to James Ferguson and his team at Signal Books for publishing this odd book, probably against all sane advice. Katie Isbester made some extremely helpful suggestions for improving the book in all sorts of ways.

Cheers also to Dan McCabe for advising on Coast of Teeth's design and layout. Also, Cecilia Le Poer Power for always insightful help on all things aesthetic.

Stephen Harper, Mike Manson, Karenanne Knight, John Bartlett and Simon Sykes all shared with us their insights into the English littoral and recommended intriguing places to visit.

We are grateful to the Faculty of Creative and Cultural Industries at the University of Portsmouth for funding several research trips during which we gathered the material inside this book.

And finally, thanks to all those in coastal communities up and down England who gave us their time and wisdom and jokes and anecdotes – in the final analysis, *Coast of Teeth* is really all about them.